NINJA C

DELUXE PROTEIN

COOKBOOK

1500 days of simples and easy plant based, diary free, low calorie, high protein ice cream, yoghurt, sorbet, milkshake & gelato for ninja creami

Avery Stoneheart

Copyright © 2024 by Avery Stoneheart

Table of Content

INTRODUCTION

Introducing the Ninja Creami Deluxe Protein Cookbook – your ultimate guide to creating delicious, healthy frozen treats with the power of the Ninja Creami Deluxe. My name is Avery Stoneheart, and I am a passionate foodie dedicated to helping others discover the joys of nutritious, mouth-watering cuisine.

The Ninja Creami Deluxe is a revolutionary kitchen appliance that allows you to create a variety of frozen desserts, including ice cream, yogurt, sorbet, milkshakes, and gelato, right in the comfort of your own home. But this isn't just any recipe book – this book focuses on creating plant-based, dairy-free, low-calorie, and high-protein treats that are both tasty and nutritious.

With my years of experience in the food industry and my love for healthy, delicious food, I have curated a collection of over 1500 days of recipes that showcase the full potential of the Ninja Creami Deluxe. Each recipe is carefully crafted to prioritize plant-based, dairy-free, low-calorie, and high-protein ingredients, ensuring that you can indulge in your favorite frozen treats without compromising your health goals.

The Ninja Creami Deluxe Protein Cookbook is designed for anyone looking to incorporate more nutritious, plant-based, and dairy-free options into their diet while still enjoying the pleasure of delicious frozen desserts. Whether you're a seasoned chef, a busy parent, or simply someone looking to try something new, this book has something for everyone.

So, let's dive into the world of Ninja Creami Deluxe and discover the endless possibilities of creating mouth-watering, healthy frozen treats. Get ready to indulge in guilt-free pleasure and take your taste buds on an unforgettable journey!

Chapter 1:

Welcome to the World of Delicious & Nutritious Frozen Treats

Hi there, my name is Avery Stoneheart, and I am thrilled to welcome you to the exciting world of nutritious and delicious frozen treats! As the author of this book, I want to share my passion for creating healthy, fl avorful frozen desserts that you can feel good about indulging in.

As a food enthusiast and health-conscious individual, I have always believed that delicious and nutritious are not mutually exclusive. With the right ingredients and the magic of the Ninja Creami Deluxe, we can create frozen treats that are both tasty and good for you. My goal is to provide you with a collection of recipes that prioritize plant-based, dairy-free, low-calorie, and high-protein options, so you can enjoy your favorite treats guilt-free.

Whether you are a seasoned chef or a beginner in the kitchen, this book offers a range of recipes that cater to all skill levels and dietary preferences. I have personally curated and tested each recipe to ensure that it meets the highest standards of taste and nutrition. From classic favorites like chocolate and vanilla ice cream to innovative creations like matcha green tea sorbet and black bean brownie yogurt, this book has something for everyone.

The Benefits of Your Bowl

The key ingredients used in these recipes, such as protein powders, nut butters, fruits, and healthy fats, offer numerous nutritional benefits that can support your overall health and wellness. *Let's dive deeper into the nutritional advantages of these key ingredients:*

Protein Powders

Protein is an essential macronutrient that plays a crucial role in muscle growth and repair, as well as supporting a healthy immune system. The protein powders used in these recipes, such as whey, casein, pea, and hemp, offer a convenient way to boost your protein intake and support your fitness and wellness goals. These protein powders also come in various flavors, allowing you to experiment with different taste profiles and create unique frozen treats that suit your preferences.

Nut Butters

Nut butters, such as almond, peanut, and cashew, are rich in healthy fats, fiber, and essential vitamins and minerals. They provide a creamy texture and nutty flavor to your frozen treats while also supporting heart health and cognitive function. In addition, nut butters are an excellent source of plant-based protein, making them a versatile and nutritious ingredient in your kitchen.

Fruits

Fruits are an essential component of a healthy diet, and the recipes in this book incorporate a variety of fruits to add natural sweetness, flavor, and essential nutrients. From berries and citrus to tropical fruits and stone fruits, these recipes showcase the versatility and benefits of incorporating fruits into your frozen treats. Fruits are an excellent source of fiber, vitamins, and antioxidants, supporting immune health, digestion, and overall wellness.

Healthy Fats

Healthy fats, such as coconut oil, avocado, and nuts, play a crucial role in maintaining optimal health and well-being. They provide essential fatty acids, support brain health, and contribute to a feeling of fullness, helping you manage your appetite and maintain a healthy weight.

Incorporating healthy fats into your frozen treats not only enhances their flavor and texture but also provides numerous health benefits. Coconut oil, for example, is a popular choice in these recipes due to its ability to remain solid at cold temperatures, providing a creamy and satisfying texture. Additionally, avocado adds a unique twist to classic desserts and provides a boost of healthy fats and fiber.

By combining these key ingredients in creative and nutritious ways, these recipes offer a range of health benefits while still satisfying your sweet tooth. Whether you are looking to boost your protein intake, support heart health, or simply enjoy a delicious frozen treat, this book has something for you.

Sweet Without the Guilt

Traditional frozen desserts often rely on added sugars, which can contribute to weight gain, tooth decay, and other health issues. However, the recipes in this book prioritize the use of healthy sweeteners and sugar substitutes that allow you to enjoy the sweet taste without the negative impacts of added sugars.

Healthy sweeteners and sugar substitutes, such as stevia, monk fruit extract, erythritol, and coconut sugar, offer a range of benefits over traditional added sugars. Stevia, for example, is a natural sweetener derived from the leaves of the Stevia rebaudiana plant, offering zero calories and a low glycemic index. Monk fruit extract, on the other hand, is another natural sweetener that is high in antioxidants and has anti-inflammatory properties.

When choosing sweeteners, it's essential to consider your personal taste preferences and any dietary restrictions. Some sweeteners may have a different taste or texture compared to traditional added sugars, so it's essential to experiment with different options to find the one that suits your preferences.

In addition to using healthy sweeteners, these recipes also incorporate natural sources of sweetness, such as fruits, to reduce the need for added sugars. By prioritizing whole, nutrient-dense ingredients, these recipes provide a healthier alternative to traditional frozen treats.

Portion Control & Mindful Eating

While the recipes in this book are designed with portion control in mind, it's essential to practice mindful eating to ensure that you are consuming the right amount of food to meet your energy needs. Mindful eating involves paying attention to your hunger and fullness cues, savoring each bite, and enjoying your food without distractions.

To support portion control, consider using smaller bowls or serving dishes and enjoying your frozen treats as a part of a balanced meal or snack. Additionally, it's essential to be mindful of your overall calorie intake and to balance your treat consumption with other nutritious foods throughout the day.

Chapter 2:

Mastering Your Ninja Creami Deluxe

Meet Your Machine

This is where we'll explore the world of the Ninja Creami Deluxe and discover how to master this amazing appliance. The Ninja Creami Deluxe is a versatile and innovative kitchen tool that allows you to create a variety of frozen desserts, including ice cream, yogurt, sorbet, milkshakes, and gelato. In this chapter, we'll take a closer look at the features and functions of this impressive machine.

Features

- The Ninja Creami Deluxe features a sleek, compact design that fits easily on your countertop.
- It is equipped with a powerful motor that quickly and efficiently churns ingredients into smooth, creamy frozen treats.
- The machine comes with a variety of interchangeable blades, including a Creami Blade for making ice cream and a Smooth Boost Blade for creating sorbet and milkshakes.
- It also includes a range of containers, including a Pint Container for making individual servings and a Quart Container for larger batches.
- The Ninja Creami Deluxe has an easy-to-use digital control panel that allows you to select your desired recipe and set the machine to work.

Functions

- The Ninja Creami Deluxe can make a wide range of frozen treats, including ice cream, yogurt, sorbet, milkshakes, and gelato.
- The machine's powerful motor churns ingredients into a smooth and creamy consistency.
- The interchangeable blades allow you to customize your frozen treats and experiment with different textures and flavors.
- The machine's digital control panel makes it easy to select your desired recipe and monitor the progress of your frozen treats.
- The Ninja Creami Deluxe's compact design makes it easy to store and easy to clean.

Freezing & Processing

Now that you've gotten acquainted with the features and functions of your Ninja Creami Deluxe, it's time to dive into the freezing and processing process. In this section, we'll provide detailed instructions on how to properly freeze your pint containers and use your machine to create delicious frozen treats.

Freezing the Pint Containers

1. Begin by preparing your ingredients according to your chosen recipe.
2. Pour the mixture into the Pint Container, leaving at least 1/2 inch of headspace at the top.
3. Seal the Pint Container tightly and place it in the freezer.

4. Allow the mixture to freeze completely, which typically takes around 24 hours.

5. Once frozen, remove the Pint Container from the freezer and let it sit at room temperature for about 10 minutes to soften slightly.

Proper Machine Usage for Different Recipe Types

Ice Cream

1. Insert the Creami Blade into the Ninja Creami Deluxe.
2. Place the frozen Pint Container into the machine and secure the lid.
3. Press the "Ice Cream" button and wait for the machine to churn the mixture into soft-serve consistency.
4. Remove the Pint Container and enjoy your ice cream as is, or place it back into the freezer for a firmer consistency.

Yogurt

1. Insert the Creami Blade into the Ninja Creami Deluxe.
2. Place the frozen Pint Container into the machine and secure the lid.
3. Press the "Yogurt" button and wait for the machine to churn the mixture into a smooth, creamy texture.
4. Remove the Pint Container and enjoy your yogurt as is, or garnish with fresh fruit or granola for added flavor and texture.

Sorbet

1. Insert the Smooth Boost Blade into the Ninja Creami Deluxe.
2. Place the frozen Pint Container into the machine and secure the lid.
3. Press the "Sorbet" button and wait for the machine to churn the mixture into a refreshing and icy treat.
4. Remove the Pint Container and enjoy your sorbet as is, or use it as a base for cocktails or smoothies.

By following these steps, you'll be able to create a variety of frozen treats with ease using your Ninja Creami Deluxe. Remember to always clean and sanitize your machine after each use to ensure the best results for your next batch.

Troubleshooting Tips

While the Ninja Creami Deluxe is a user-friendly appliance, you may encounter some issues during its operation. In this section, we'll cover some common issues and offer solutions to help you troubleshoot and maintain your machine for smooth operation.

Issue: Machine Won't Turn On
Solution: Check that the machine is plugged into a working outlet and that the power switch is turned on. If the machine still won't turn on, contact Ninja customer service for assistance.

Issue: Mixture Is Too Thick
Solution: If the mixture in the Pint Container is too thick, the machine may have difficulty churning it properly. Try thawing the mixture slightly by letting it sit at room temperature for a few minutes before placing it back in the freezer. You can also add a splash of milk or cream to the mixture to help thin it out.

Issue: Mixture Is Too Thin
Solution: If the mixture in the Pint Container is too thin, the machine may not be able to churn it into a creamy texture. Try freezing the mixture for an additional hour or two before placing it in the machine. You can also try increasing the amount of cream or reducing the amount of liquid in the mixture to help thicken it up.

Issue: Machine Is Noisy
Solution: The Ninja Creami Deluxe may make some noise while in operation, but excessive noise could indicate an issue. Check that the Pint Container is properly seated in the machine and that

the blade is securely attached. If the noise persists, contact Ninja customer service for assistance.

Issue: Cleaning and Maintenance
Solution: Regular cleaning and maintenance are essential for keeping your Ninja Creami Deluxe in top working order. Always clean the machine thoroughly after each use, following the manufacturer's instructions. Make sure to clean and sanitize all removable parts, including the Pint Containers and blades.

By following these troubleshooting tips, you can ensure that your Ninja Creami Deluxe continues to operate smoothly and efficiently, allowing you to create delicious frozen treats with ease

Building Your Pantry

Having a well-stocked pantry is crucial for creating delicious frozen treats with ease. Here are some healthy ingredients to keep on hand to ensure you always have what you need to make your favorite recipes.

Protein Powders

1. Whey protein powder: A popular choice among fitness enthusiasts, whey protein provides a high-quality source of protein and can be used in a variety of frozen treats.
2. Plant-based protein powder: For those following a vegan or dairy-free diet, plant-based protein powders like pea, hemp, or soy are excellent alternatives to whey protein.
3. Collagen peptides: A popular ingredient in health and wellness circles, collagen peptides support skin, joint, and gut health and can be easily incorporated into your frozen treats.

Nut Butters

1. Almond butter: A versatile nut butter that adds a rich, creamy texture to your frozen treats.
2. Peanut butter: A classic favorite that offers a familiar and comforting flavor profile.
3. Cashew butter: A smooth and mild nut butter that blends well with other flavors and is ideal for those with nut allergies.

Fruits

1. Bananas: A staple ingredient in many frozen dessert recipes, bananas provide natural sweetness and a creamy texture.
2. Berries: A versatile fruit option that adds a burst of flavor and color to your frozen treats.
3. Mango: A tropical fruit that offers a unique flavor and can be used in a variety of recipes.

Healthy Sweeteners and Sugar Substitutes

1. Stevia: A natural sweetener derived from the leaves of the Stevia rebaudiana plant, stevia offers zero calories and a low glycemic index.
2. Monk fruit extract: Another natural sweetener that is high in antioxidants and has anti-inflammatory properties.
3. Coconut sugar: A natural sweetener that provides a lower glycemic index than refined sugar and a subtle caramel-like flavor.

By keeping these healthy ingredients on hand, you'll be able to create a variety of frozen treats with ease, knowing that you're incorporating nutritious and delicious components into your recipes. Experiment with different combinations and flavor profiles to find your perfect match.

Chapter 3:

The Foundation of Flavor
Base Recipes

We'll delve into the foundation of flavor by exploring a variety of base recipes that serve as the building blocks for your frozen treats. In this section, we'll start by focusing on protein-rich options that offer both taste and nutrition. Let's begin with some Protein Powerhouses: Vanilla Protein Soft Serve, Chocolate Protein Ice Cream, and Peanut Butter Protein Smoothie Bowl Base.

Vanilla Protein Soft Serve

This creamy and refreshing soft serve is a delicious way to boost your protein intake while satisfying your sweet tooth. The addition of vanilla protein powder provides a subtle sweetness and a rich, velvety texture.

Ingredients

- 2 frozen bananas
- 1 scoop of vanilla protein powder
- 1/4 cup of unsweetened almond milk
- 1/2 teaspoon of vanilla extract

Instructions

1. Place the frozen bananas, vanilla protein powder, almond milk, and vanilla extract into the Ninja Creami Deluxe's Pint Container.
2. Seal the container tightly and freeze for at least 24 hours.
3. Once frozen, remove the container from the freezer and let it sit at room temperature for about 10 minutes to soften slightly.
4. Insert the Creami Blade into the machine, place the container in the machine, and secure the lid.
5. Press the "Ice Cream" button and wait for the machine to churn the mixture into soft-serve consistency.
6. Enjoy your Vanilla Protein Soft Serve as is or add your favorite toppings, such as fresh berries, nuts, or dark chocolate chips.

Chocolate Protein Ice Cream

This decadent and creamy ice cream is a chocolate lover's dream, packed with rich cocoa flavor and protein-rich ingredients.

Ingredients

- 2 frozen bananas
- 1 scoop of chocolate protein powder
- 1/4 cup of unsweetened almond milk
- 2 tablespoons of cocoa powder
- 1 teaspoon of honey or maple syrup (optional)

Instructions

1. Place the frozen bananas, chocolate protein powder, almond milk, cocoa powder, and optional sweetener into the Ninja Creami Deluxe's Pint Container.
2. Seal the container tightly and freeze for at least 24 hours.
3. Once frozen, remove the container from the freezer and let it sit at room temperature for about 10 minutes to soften slightly.
4. Insert the Creami Blade into the machine, place the container in the machine, and secure the lid.
5. Press the "Ice Cream" button and wait for the machine to churn the mixture into a smooth and creamy consistency.
6. Enjoy your Chocolate Protein Ice Cream as is or garnish with chocolate chips, whipped cream, or a drizzle of chocolate sauce.

Peanut Butter Protein Smoothie Bowl Base

This creamy and indulgent smoothie bowl base combines the nutty richness of peanut butter with the nutritional benefits of protein powder. It's the perfect foundation for creating a variety of healthy and delicious smoothie bowls.

Ingredients

- 1 frozen banana
- 1/2 cup of plain Greek yogurt
- 1 scoop of vanilla or chocolate protein powder
- 2 tablespoons of natural peanut butter
- 1/4 cup of unsweetened almond milk

Instructions

1. Place the frozen banana, Greek yogurt, protein powder, peanut butter, and almond milk into the Ninja Creami Deluxe's Pint Container.
2. Seal the container tightly and freeze for at least 24 hours.
3. Once frozen, remove the container from the freezer and let it sit at room temperature for about 10 minutes to soften slightly.
4. Insert the Creami Blade into the machine, place the container in the machine, and secure the lid.
5. Press the "Smooth Boost" button and wait for the machine to churn the mixture into a thick and creamy base.
6. Enjoy your Peanut Butter Protein Smoothie Bowl Base as is, or top with fresh fruit, granola, nuts, seeds, and other toppings of your choice.

These Protein Powerhouse base recipes offer a variety of flavors and textures to suit your taste preferences while providing essential nutrients and satisfying your sweet tooth. Feel free to experiment with different protein powders, nut butters, and flavorings to create your own unique versions of these frozen treats.

Variations and Customization

Each of these base recipes can be customized to suit your personal taste preferences and dietary needs. Here are a few ideas for variations:

Vanilla Protein Soft Serve: Add a splash of coconut extract for a tropical twist or mix in some fresh berries for added texture and flavor.

Chocolate Protein Ice Cream: Try using different types of protein powder, such as plant-based or casein, to change the flavor and texture. You can also experiment with different types of nut butters, such as almond or cashew, for added richness.

Peanut Butter Protein Smoothie Bowl Base: Use different types of nut butters, such as almond or cashew, to switch up the flavor. You can also experiment with different types of protein powder, such as pea or hemp, to change the nutritional profile.

By experimenting with different variations, you can create endless possibilities for delicious and nutritious frozen treats using your Ninja Creami Deluxe.

Sorbet made from watermelon and mint

Cool down on a hot summer day with this refreshing and light sorbet made from watermelon and mint. This recipe is perfect for those looking for a guilt-free dessert option that still satisfies their sweet tooth.

Ingredients

- 4 cups of cubed seedless watermelon
- 1/4 cup of fresh mint leaves
- 1/4 cup of lime juice
- 1/4 cup of honey or agave nectar

Instructions

1. Place the watermelon, mint leaves, lime juice, and honey or agave nectar into a blender and blend until smooth.
2. Strain the mixture through a fine-mesh sieve to remove any solids.
3. Pour the mixture into the Ninja Creami Deluxe's Pint Container.
4. Seal the container tightly and freeze for at least 24 hours.
5. Once frozen, remove the container from the freezer and let it sit at room temperature for about 10 minutes to soften slightly.
6. Insert the Smooth Boost Blade into the machine, place the container in the machine, and secure the lid.
7. Press the "Sorbet" button and wait for the machine to churn the mixture into a refreshing and minty sorbet.
8. Enjoy your Refreshing Watermelon Mint Sorbet as is, or garnish with fresh mint leaves and a sprinkle of lime zest for added brightness and flavor.

9. This sorbet is a great way to use up leftover watermelon and is sure to become a summertime favorite. The combination of sweet watermelon and refreshing mint makes for a perfect treat on a hot day.

Creamy Mango Sorbet Variations

1. Mango-Strawberry Sorbet: Add 1 cup of frozen strawberries to the mix for a fruity twist.
2. Mango-Lime Sorbet: Replace the honey or maple syrup with 1/4 cup of freshly squeezed lime juice for a tangy and refreshing flavor.
3. Mango-Coconut Sorbet: Replace the almond milk with 1/4 cup of unsweetened coconut milk for a tropical twist.

Tropical Pineapple Dole Whip Variations

Pineapple-Banana Dole Whip: Add 1 frozen banana to the mix for a creamier texture and flavor.

Pineapple-Coconut Dole Whip: Replace the coconut milk with 1/2 cup of unsweetened coconut cream for an even more tropical flavor.

Pineapple-Mango Dole Whip: Replace half of the pineapple chunks with frozen mango chunks for a blend of tropical flavors.

Refreshing Watermelon Mint Sorbet Variations

1. Watermelon-Lime Sorbet: Replace the mint leaves with 1/4 cup of freshly squeezed lime juice for a tangy and refreshing flavor.
2. Watermelon-Basil Sorbet: Replace the mint leaves with 1/4 cup of fresh basil leaves for a unique and herby flavor.
3. Watermelon-Strawberry Sorbet: Add 1 cup of frozen strawberries to the mix for a sweet and fruity twist.

By experimenting with different ingredients and flavor combinations, you can create endless possibilities for delicious frozen treats using your Ninja Creami Deluxe. Have fun customizing these recipes to suit your taste preferences and dietary needs!

Creamy Classics

In this section, we'll explore some classic frozen treat recipes with a healthy twist. These Creamy Classics include Plant-Based Yogurt, Dairy-Free Mocha Gelato, and a Healthy Chocolate Milkshake Base. These recipes offer a variety of options for those with dietary restrictions or those simply looking to incorporate more nutritious ingredients into their treats.

Plant-Based Yogurt

This recipe is a great alternative to traditional dairy yogurt, offering a creamy and tangy texture and flavor without the use of animal products. It's a versatile base that can be customized with various mix-ins and toppings to suit your taste preferences.

Ingredients

- 1 cup of cashews, soaked overnight and drained
- 1 cup of plant-based milk (such as almond or coconut milk)
- 1 tablespoon of lemon juice
- 1/2 teaspoon of vanilla extract
- 1/4 cup of maple syrup or honey (optional, for sweetening)

Instructions

- Place the soaked and drained cashews, plant-based milk, lemon juice, and vanilla extract into a high-speed blender.
1. Blend until smooth and creamy, scraping down the sides as needed.
2. If desired, add maple syrup or honey for added sweetness.
3. Pour the mixture into the Ninja Creami Deluxe's Pint Container.
4. Seal the container tightly and freeze for at least 24 hours.
5. Once frozen, remove the container from the freezer and let it sit at room temperature for about 10 minutes to soften slightly.
6. Insert the Smooth Boost Blade into the machine, place the container in the machine, and secure the lid.
7. Press the "Smooth Boost" button and wait for the machine to churn the mixture into a creamy and tangy plant-based yogurt.
8. Enjoy your Plant-Based Yogurt as is, or garnish with fresh berries, granola, or nuts for added texture and flavor.

Dairy-Free Mocha Gelato

This rich and creamy gelato is perfect for coffee lovers looking for a dairy-free alternative. The combination of chocolate and coffee creates a sophisticated and indulgent treat that's sure to satisfy your sweet tooth.

Ingredients

- 1 cup of canned coconut milk
- 1/4 cup of brewed coffee, cooled
- 2 tablespoons of cocoa powder
- 1/4 cup of maple syrup or honey
- 1 teaspoon of vanilla extract

Instructions

1. Place the coconut milk, brewed coffee, cocoa powder, maple syrup or honey, and vanilla extract into a blender.
2. Blend until smooth and well combined.
3. Pour the mixture into the Ninja Creami Deluxe's Pint Container.
4. Seal the container tightly and freeze for at least 24 hours.
5. Once frozen, remove the container from the freezer and let it sit at room temperature for about 10 minutes to soften slightly.
6. Insert the Smooth Boost Blade into the machine, place the container in the machine, and secure the lid.
7. Press the "Gelato" button and wait for the machine to churn the mixture into a creamy and indulgent dairy-free gelato.
8. Enjoy your Dairy-Free Mocha Gelato as is, or garnish with shaved dark chocolate, espresso beans, or whipped coconut cream for added richness and texture.

Healthy Chocolate Milkshake Base

This recipe offers a healthier alternative to traditional chocolate milkshakes, using nut butter and banana to create a creamy and satisfying base. It's a great option for those looking to incorporate more nutritious ingredients into their treats without sacrificing taste.

Ingredients

- 1 frozen banana
- 1/4 cup of natural nut butter (such as peanut or almond butter)
- 1/2 cup of plant-based milk (such as almond or coconut milk)
- 1 tablespoon of cocoa powder
- 1 tablespoon of honey or maple syrup (optional, for sweetening)

Instructions

1. Place the frozen banana, nut butter, plant-based milk, cocoa powder, and optional sweetener into a blender.
2. Blend until smooth and creamy, scraping down the sides as needed.
3. Pour the mixture into the Ninja Creami Deluxe's Pint Container.
4. Seal the container tightly and freeze for at least 24 hours.
5. Once frozen, remove the container from the freezer and let it sit at room temperature for about 10 minutes to soften slightly.
6. Insert the Smooth Boost Blade into the machine, place the container in the machine, and secure the lid.

7. Press the "Smooth Boost" button and wait for the machine to churn the mixture into a rich and creamy healthy chocolate milkshake base.
8. Enjoy your Healthy Chocolate Milkshake Base as is, or add mix-ins such as fresh berries, chia seeds, or hemp hearts for added nutrition and flavor.

These Creamy Classics offer a variety of options for creating delicious and nutritious frozen treats using your Ninja Creami Deluxe. By experimenting with different ingredients and flavor combinations, you can customize these recipes to suit your taste preferences and dietary needs while still enjoying the indulgent taste of classic treats.

Plant-Based Yogurt Variations

1. Blueberry-Lemon Plant-Based Yogurt: Add 1/2 cup of frozen blueberries and the zest of 1 lemon to the base recipe.
2. Strawberry-Basil Plant-Based Yogurt: Replace the vanilla extract with 1/4 cup of fresh basil leaves and add 1 cup of frozen strawberries to the base recipe.
3. Vanilla-Coconut Plant-Based Yogurt: Add 1/2 teaspoon of coconut extract to the base recipe for added tropical flavor.

Dairy-Free Mocha Gelato Variations

1. Salted Caramel-Mocha Gelato: Add 2 tablespoons of salted caramel sauce to the base recipe for a sweet and savory twist.
2. Mint-Chocolate Gelato: Replace the cocoa powder with 1/4 cup of fresh mint leaves and add 2 tablespoons of mini chocolate chips to the base recipe.
3. Coffee-Banana Gelato: Add 1 frozen banana to the base recipe for added sweetness and creaminess.

Healthy Chocolate Milkshake Base Variations

1. Chocolate-Peanut Butter Milkshake: Add 1/4 cup of natural peanut butter to the base recipe for added protein and flavor.
2. Chocolate-Cherry Milkshake: Add 1 cup of frozen cherries to the base recipe for a sweet and tangy twist.
3. Chocolate-Hazelnut Milkshake: Replace the nut butter with 1/4 cup of hazelnut butter for a classic chocolate-hazelnut flavor.

By experimenting with different ingredients and flavor combinations, you can create endless possibilities for delicious and nutritious frozen treats using your Ninja Creami Deluxe. Have fun customizing these recipes to suit your taste preferences and dietary needs while still enjoying the indulgent taste of classic treats.

Mix-Ins: Crunchy Delights

Adding mix-ins to your frozen treats is an excellent way to enhance the flavor, texture, and nutritional value of your creations. In this section, we'll explore some Crunchy Delights: Granola & Nut Clusters, Homemade Chocolate Chips & Cacao Nibs, and Seeds & Toasted Coconut. These mix-ins offer a variety of options for adding crunch and depth to your frozen treats while
boosting their nutritional value.

Granola & Nut Clusters

These homemade granola and nut clusters are an excellent addition to frozen yogurt, ice cream, and smoothie bowls. They provide a satisfying crunch and a boost of nutrients, making them a delicious and nutritious mix-in option.

Ingredients

- 1 cup of rolled oats
- 1/2 cup of mixed nuts (such as almonds, pecans, and walnuts)
- 2 tablespoons of coconut oil
- 2 tablespoons of honey or maple syrup
- 1 teaspoon of cinnamon (optional)

Instructions

1. Preheat the oven to 350°F (175°C) and line a baking sheet with parchment paper.
2. In a medium bowl, combine the rolled oats, mixed nuts, coconut oil, honey or maple syrup, and optional cinnamon.
3. Mix well until all the ingredients are evenly coated.
4. Spread the mixture evenly on the prepared baking sheet.
5. Bake for 10-15 minutes, stirring halfway through, until the granola and nuts are golden brown and toasted.
6. Let the granola and nut clusters cool completely before storing in an airtight container for later use as mix-ins for your frozen treats.

Homemade Chocolate Chips & Cacao Nibs

These homemade chocolate chips and cacao nibs offer a rich and decadent mix-in option for your frozen treats. They're easy to make and provide a boost of antioxidants and nutrients.

Ingredients

- 1/2 cup of dark chocolate chips or chopped dark chocolate
- 1/4 cup of raw cacao nibs

Instructions

1. Place the dark chocolate chips or chopped dark chocolate in a heat-resistant bowl.
2. Melt the chocolate in the microwave in short intervals, stirring frequently, or over a double boiler.
3. Once melted, stir in the raw cacao nibs until evenly combined.
4. Spread the mixture evenly on a parchment-lined baking sheet.
5. Let the mixture cool completely, then break it into small pieces to create homemade chocolate chips and cacao nibs.
6. Store the mix-ins in an airtight container for later use in your frozen treats.

Seeds & Toasted Coconut

This mix-in option provides a nutty and crunchy texture, as well as a boost of healthy fats and nutrients. It's an excellent addition to smoothie bowls, frozen yogurt, and ice cream.

Ingredients

- 1/4 cup of pumpkin seeds
- 1/4 cup of sunflower seeds
- 1/4 cup of shredded unsweetened coconut

Instructions

1. Preheat the oven to 350°F (175°C) and line a baking sheet with parchment paper.
2. Spread the pumpkin seeds, sunflower seeds, and shredded coconut evenly on the prepared baking sheet.
3. Bake for 5-10 minutes, stirring halfway through, until the seeds and coconut are toasted and golden brown.
4. Let the mix-ins cool completely before storing in an airtight container for later use in your frozen treats.

These Crunchy Delights: Granola & Nut Clusters, Homemade Chocolate Chips & Cacao Nibs, and Seeds & Toasted Coconut offer a variety of options for adding texture and flavor to your frozen treats while boosting their nutritional value. Feel free to experiment with different nuts, seeds, and flavorings to create your own unique mix-ins.

Frozen Yogurt with Granola & Nut Clusters

For a simple and nutritious frozen treat, combine your favorite plant-based yogurt with the Granola & Nut Clusters mix-in. Follow the instructions for the Plant-Based Yogurt recipe in the Creamy Classics section, and fold in the Granola & Nut Clusters before churning the mixture in the Ninja Creami Deluxe. Top with additional clusters and fresh berries for a nutritious and delicious frozen yogurt treat.

Chocolate-Covered Strawberry Ice Cream with Cacao Nibs

For a decadent and antioxidant-rich frozen treat, combine your favorite chocolate ice cream recipe with fresh strawberries and the Homemade Chocolate Chips & Cacao Nibs mix-in. Follow the instructions for the Dairy-Free Mocha Gelato recipe in the Creamy Classics section, and fold in chopped fresh strawberries and the Homemade Chocolate Chips & Cacao Nibs before churning the mixture in the Ninja Creami Deluxe. Serve with additional nibs and a drizzle of melted dark chocolate for a chocolate-covered strawberry ice cream treat that's both indulgent and nutritious.

Mango-Pineapple Smoothie Bowl with Toasted Coconut

For a refreshing and tropical smoothie bowl, combine your favorite mango and pineapple smoothie recipe with the Seeds & Toasted Coconut mix-in. Follow the instructions for the Refreshing Watermelon Mint Sorbet recipe in the Fruity Delights section, and adjust the ingredients to include frozen mango and pineapple instead of watermelon and mint. Blend the mixture until smooth and creamy, then fold in the Seeds & Toasted Coconut mix-in before serving. Top with additional toasted coconut, sliced kiwi, and fresh mint for a vibrant and nutritious smoothie bowl.

Fruity Flavors

In this section, we'll explore some Fruity Flavors to incorporate into your frozen treats. These mix-ins include Fresh Berries & Sliced Fruits, Frozen Fruit Purees & Swirls, and Homemade Fruit Jams & Sauces. These fruity flavors offer a variety of options for adding natural sweetness and a burst of flavor to your frozen treats while boosting their nutritional value.

Fresh Berries & Sliced Fruits

Adding fresh fruits to your frozen treats is an easy and delicious way to incorporate more nutrients and fiber into your diet. Here are some ideas for incorporating fresh fruits into your frozen treats:

1. Fold in sliced strawberries, blueberries, raspberries, or blackberries into your yogurt or ice cream base.
2. Top your frozen yogurt or smoothie bowl with sliced mango, pineapple, or banana for a fresh and colorful garnish.
3. Create a strawberry or raspberry swirl in your ice cream by blending fresh berries with a little honey or maple syrup, then swirling it into the ice cream before freezing.

Frozen Fruit Purees & Swirls

Creating frozen fruit purees and swirls is a great way to add intense fruit flavor and a pop of color to your frozen treats. Here are some ideas for incorporating frozen fruit purees and swirls into your frozen treats:

1. Blend frozen berries or tropical fruits like mango or pineapple with a little honey or maple syrup to create a

thick puree. Swirl this puree into your ice cream or yogurt base before freezing.

2. Freeze mashed bananas, mangoes, or other fruits into small chunks, then fold them into your frozen yogurt or ice cream for a burst of intense fruit flavor.

3. Create a fruit sauce by cooking down fresh or frozen berries or tropical fruits with a little sugar and lemon juice. Once cooled, swirl this sauce into your frozen treats for added flavor and color.

Homemade Fruit Jams & Sauces

Making your own fruit jams and sauces is a great way to control the amount of sugar and preservatives in your frozen treats. Here are some ideas for incorporating homemade fruit jams and sauces into your frozen treats:

1. Cook down fresh or frozen berries or tropical fruits with a little sugar and lemon juice to create a thick jam. Fold this jam into your ice cream or yogurt base before freezing, or use it as a swirl in your frozen treats.

2. Create a fruit coulis by blending fresh or frozen berries or tropical fruits with a little sugar and lemon juice. Use this coulis as a swirl in your frozen treats, or serve it as a sauce over your ice cream or yogurt for added flavor and color.

Flavorful Additions

Sometimes, the key to elevating your frozen treats is in the details. Adding spices, extracts, nut butters, and protein powders can take your frozen yogurt, ice cream, and smoothie bowls to the next level. These Flavorful Additions offer a variety of options for boosting the flavor and nutritional profile of your frozen treats.

Spices

Spices like cinnamon and cardamom add a warm and aromatic flavor to frozen yogurt and ice cream. They can also enhance the natural sweetness of fruit purees and swirls, making your frozen treats taste even more decadent.

- Cinnamon: Use cinnamon powder or freshly ground cinnamon sticks to add a warm, sweet spice flavor to your frozen treats.
- Cardamom: Ground cardamom has a warm, floral, and slightly citrusy flavor that pairs well with chocolate or tropical fruits in frozen treats.

Extracts

Extracts like vanilla and mint add depth of flavor to your frozen treats, making them taste more sophisticated and complex.
Here are some extracts that can be used in frozen treats:

- Vanilla extract: Vanilla extract adds a warm, sweet flavor to frozen treats, making them taste richer and more decadent.

- Mint extract: Mint extract adds a refreshing, cool flavor to frozen treats, making them taste more refreshing and invigorating.
- Almond extract: Almond extract adds a nutty and slightly sweet flavor to frozen treats, making them taste more complex and sophisticated.
- Coffee extract: Coffee extract adds a rich, roasted flavor to frozen treats, making them taste more indulgent and sophisticated.

Nut Butters

Nut butters such as peanut butter, almond butter, and cashew butter add a creamy and protein-packed element to your frozen treats. They can be used to enhance the flavor and nutritional value of yogurt, ice cream, and smoothie bowls.

Protein Powders

Protein powders can be added to frozen yogurt and smoothie bowls to boost their protein content while still keeping them creamy and delicious. Look for protein powders made from plant-based sources like hemp, pea, or rice, which can be blended into frozen treats for a nutrient-packed boost.

Chapter 4:

50 Days of Frozen Fun

Frozen treats are not only delicious, but they can also be nutritious. In this chapter, we'll explore a variety of recipes that are both tasty and healthy, using the Ninja Creami Deluxe to create unique and indulgent frozen treats. We'll divide the 50 recipes into sections based on the base recipe and provide eye-catching titles, easy-to-follow instructions, nutritional information, customization tips, and beautiful photos for each recipe.

Protein Ice Creams

Cookies & Cream Dream Ice Cream

A classic combination of creamy protein ice cream studded with crunchy chocolate cookie bits.

Ingredients (serves 1):

- ½ cup frozen banana chunks
- ¼ cup frozen Greek yogurt
- ¼ cup unsweetened vanilla almond milk
- 1 tbsp cocoa powder
- 1 scoop chocolate protein powder
- ¼ cup chopped dark chocolate cookies

Prep Time: 5 minutes

Instructions:

1. Combine all ingredients except the cookies in your Ninja Creami.
2. Process according to manufacturer's instructions until thick and creamy.
3. Fold in the chopped cookies and serve immediately.

Nutrition (per serving):

- Calories: 300
- Protein: 20g
- Carbs: 30g
- Fat: 10g

Tips:

- Use different protein powders or mix in peanut butter for a twist.
- Substitute chopped nuts or pretzels for the cookies.

Chocolate Peanut Butter Protein Ice Cream

A classic flavor combination gets a protein-packed twist! This creamy ice cream is bursting with peanut butter flavor and rich chocolate notes, making it a delicious and satisfying treat.

Prep Time: 5 minutes

Ingredients (serves 1):

- ½ cup frozen banana chunks
- ¼ cup unsweetened vanilla almond milk
- 1 scoop chocolate protein powder
- 2 tbsp smooth peanut butter
- 1 tbsp unsweetened cocoa powder
- 1 tbsp chopped dark chocolate (optional)

Instructions:

1. Combine all ingredients except the optional dark chocolate in your Ninja Creami.
2. Process according to manufacturer's instructions until thick and creamy.
3. Fold in the chopped dark chocolate (if using) and serve immediately.

Nutrition (per serving):

- Calories: 350
- Protein: 25g
- Carbs: 30g
- Fat: 15g

Tips:

- Use a different protein powder flavor like vanilla or peanut butter for a twist.
- Substitute frozen Greek yogurt for some of the banana for added protein and creaminess.
- Add a pinch of sea salt for a flavor boost.
- Top with additional peanut butter, chopped nuts, or berries for extra indulgence.

Strawberry Banana Protein Ice Cream

A refreshing and healthy spin on the classic strawberry banana smoothie, this protein ice cream is packed with flavor and nutrients. Perfect for satisfying your sweet tooth while keeping you fueled!

Prep Time: 5 minutes

Ingredients (serves 1):

- 1 cup frozen strawberries
- 1/2 cup frozen banana chunks
- 1/4 cup unsweetened almond milk or other plant-based milk
- 1 scoop unflavored protein powder
- 1/2 tbsp honey or maple syrup (optional)
- 1/4 tsp vanilla extract (optional)

Instructions:

1. Combine all ingredients in your Ninja Creami.
2. Process according to manufacturer's instructions until smooth and creamy.
3. If desired, add a dollop of Greek yogurt or whipped cream for extra protein and richness.
4. Serve immediately and enjoy!

Nutrition (per serving - without optional toppings):

- Calories: 250
- Protein: 15g
- Carbs: 30g
- Fat: 5g

Tips:

- Use frozen yogurt instead of milk for a thicker and creamier texture.
- If you prefer a tart flavor, omit the sweetener.
- Add a squeeze of fresh lemon juice for a brighter taste.
- For a tropical twist, substitute mango for the strawberries.
- Top with sliced fresh strawberries, bananas, or granola for added texture and flavor.

Mint Chocolate Chip Protein Ice Cream

Description: Indulge in a refreshing and invigorating treat with this protein-packed mint chocolate chip ice cream. Creamy vanilla ice cream infused with cool mint and studded with dark chocolate chips for a satisfying and healthy dessert.

Prep Time: 5 minutes

Ingredients (serves 1):

- ½ cup frozen banana chunks
- ¼ cup unsweetened vanilla almond milk
- 1 scoop chocolate protein powder
- 1 tbsp unsweetened cocoa powder
- ½ tsp peppermint extract
- ¼ tsp vanilla extract
- ¼ cup mini dark chocolate chips
- Green food coloring (optional)

Instructions:

1. Combine banana chunks, almond milk, protein powder, cocoa powder, peppermint extract, and vanilla extract in your Ninja Creami.
2. Add 2-3 drops of green food coloring if desired for a vibrant mint hue.
3. Process according to manufacturer's instructions until thick and creamy.
4. Fold in the mini chocolate chips just before serving.

Nutrition (per serving):

- Calories: 300
- Protein: 20g
- Carbs: 30g
- Fat: 10g

Tips:

- Substitute frozen spinach for some of the banana for a hidden veggie boost.
- Use a different protein powder flavor like mint chocolate chip for an intensified minty experience.
- Add a pinch of sea salt for a flavor enhancement.
- Drizzle with chocolate syrup or top with additional dark chocolate shavings for extra decadence.
- For a more intense mint flavor, add a few additional drops of peppermint extract to taste.

Vanilla Chai Protein Ice Cream

Escape to a warm and comforting haven with this protein-packed vanilla chai ice cream. The creamy vanilla base melds beautifully with the aromatic spices of chai, creating a unique and satisfyingly sweet treat.

Prep Time: 5 minutes

Ingredients (serves 1):

- ½ cup frozen cauliflower florets (steamed and frozen)
- ¼ cup unsweetened almond milk
- 1 scoop vanilla protein powder
- 1 tsp ground cinnamon
- ½ tsp ground ginger
- ¼ tsp ground cardamom
- Pinch of ground cloves
- ¼ tsp vanilla extract
- 1 tbsp chopped almonds (optional)
- Drizzle of honey or maple syrup (optional)

Instructions:

1. Combine frozen cauliflower, almond milk, protein powder, spices, and vanilla extract in your Ninja Creami.
2. Process according to manufacturer's instructions until smooth and creamy.
3. Top with chopped almonds and a drizzle of honey or maple syrup (optional) for extra flavor and texture.
4. Serve immediately and enjoy!

Nutrition (per serving - without optional toppings):

- Calories: 220
- Protein: 20g
- Carbs: 20g
- Fat: 5g

Tips:

- Use steamable frozen riced cauliflower for a quicker prep.
- Substitute frozen zucchini or butternut squash for cauliflower for a different flavor profile.
- Swap vanilla protein powder for unflavored and add extra vanilla extract for more control over sweetness.
- Steep 1-2 chai tea bags in the almond milk for a more intense chai flavor.
- Sprinkle with a pinch of cayenne pepper for a subtle kick.
- Top with fresh berries or a dollop of Greek yogurt for added nutrients and taste.

Espresso Protein Ice Cream

Wake up your taste buds with this invigoratingly rich and creamy espresso protein ice cream. The perfect treat for coffee lovers, this recipe packs a protein punch while delivering a delicious shot of espresso flavor.

Prep Time: 5 minutes

Ingredients (serves 1):

- ½ cup frozen banana chunks
- ¼ cup unsweetened vanilla almond milk
- 1 scoop chocolate protein powder (or unflavored + 1 tbsp cocoa powder)
- 1 tbsp instant espresso powder
- 1 tbsp unsweetened cocoa powder (optional)
- 1 tbsp dark chocolate shavings (optional)

Instructions:

1. Combine frozen banana chunks, almond milk, protein powder, and instant espresso powder in your Ninja Creami.
2. If using, add the cocoa powder for an extra chocolatey depth.
3. Process according to manufacturer's instructions until thick and creamy.
4. Fold in the dark chocolate shavings just before serving (optional).

Nutrition (per serving):

- Calories: 300
- Protein: 20g
- Carbs: 30g
- Fat: 10g

Tips:

- Substitute frozen spinach for some of the banana for a hidden veggie boost.
- Use a different protein powder flavor like mocha or caramel for a twist.
- Add a pinch of sea salt for a flavor enhancement.
- Drizzle with caramel sauce or top with chopped biscotti for an indulgent dessert.
- For a more intense coffee flavor, add an additional ½ teaspoon of instant espresso powder.
- Substitute strong brewed coffee for some of the almond milk for a richer coffee taste.

Chocolate Hazelnut Protein Ice Cream: A Dreamy Delight

Indulge in the irresistible combination of rich chocolate and nutty hazelnut in this protein-packed ice cream! Creamy, decadent, and perfect for satisfying your sweet tooth without compromising on nutrition.

Prep Time: 5 minutes

Ingredients (serves 1):

- ½ cup frozen banana chunks
- ¼ cup unsweetened vanilla almond milk
- 1 scoop chocolate protein powder
- 1 tbsp unsweetened cocoa powder
- 1 tbsp hazelnut butter
- 1 tbsp chopped hazelnuts (optional)

Instructions:

1. Combine frozen banana chunks, almond milk, protein powder, cocoa powder, and hazelnut butter in your Ninja Creami.
2. Process according to manufacturer's instructions until thick and creamy.
3. Fold in the chopped hazelnuts just before serving (optional).

Nutrition (per serving):

- Calories: 350
- Protein: 25g
- Carbs: 30g
- Fat: 15g

Tips:

- Use frozen Greek yogurt instead of some of the banana for a thicker and creamier texture.
- If you prefer a less intense hazelnut flavor, start with ½ tablespoon of hazelnut butter and adjust to your taste.
- Add a pinch of sea salt for a flavor boost.
- Drizzle with chocolate syrup or top with additional chopped hazelnuts, berries, or cocoa nibs for extra indulgence.
- Substitute roasted butternut squash or sweet potato for the banana for a different flavor profile.
- Use a coffee protein powder instead of chocolate for a mocha-hazelnut twist.

Lemon Coconut Protein Ice Cream: Sunshine in a Bowl

Escape to the tropics with this refreshing and zesty lemon coconut protein ice cream. Creamy coconut base infused with bright lemon flavor creates a vibrant and delicious frozen treat perfect for any day.

Prep Time: 5 minutes

Ingredients (serves 1):

- ½ cup frozen banana chunks
- ¼ cup unsweetened coconut milk
- 1 scoop vanilla protein powder
- 1 tbsp lemon juice
- 1 tsp finely grated lemon zest
- 1 tbsp shredded unsweetened coconut (optional)

Instructions:

1. Combine frozen banana chunks, coconut milk, protein powder, lemon juice, and lemon zest in your Ninja Creami.
2. Process according to manufacturer's instructions until thick and creamy.
3. Fold in the shredded coconut just before serving (optional).

Nutrition (per serving):

- Calories: 250
- Protein: 20g
- Carbs: 25g
- Fat: 10g

Tips:

- Substitute frozen pineapple or mango for the banana for a tropical twist.
- Use a different protein powder flavor like coconut or lemon for a more intense flavor.
- Add a pinch of sea salt for a flavor enhancement.
- Drizzle with honey or agave nectar for added sweetness.
- Top with fresh berries, mint leaves, or additional shredded coconut for extra texture and flavor.
- For a richer coconut flavor, use full-fat coconut milk.
- Substitute frozen zucchini or cauliflower for the banana for a hidden veggie boost.

Tropical Paradise Ice Cream

A refreshing blend of mango, pineapple, and coconut for a taste of the tropics.

Ingredients (serves 1):

- ½ cup frozen mango chunks
- ½ cup frozen pineapple chunks
- ¼ cup unsweetened coconut milk
- 1 scoop unflavored protein powder
- 1 tbsp shredded coconut

Prep Time: 5 minutes

Instructions:

1. Combine all ingredients in your Ninja Creami.
2. Process according to manufacturer's instructions until thick and creamy.
3. Top with additional shredded coconut and serve immediately.

Nutrition (per serving): Calories: 250

- Protein: 15g
- Carbs: 35g
- Fat: 5g

Tips:

- Add a drizzle of lime juice for an extra zing.
- Substitute other tropical fruits, like papaya or kiwi.
- Remember to use the same format for the remaining 8 Protein Ice Cream recipes with unique titles, descriptions, ingredients, instructions, nutritional information, and tips.

SORBETS

Berry Burst Sorbet: A Symphony of Summer Fruit

Explode with flavor with this vibrant and refreshing berry burst sorbet! Packed with antioxidant-rich berries and bursting with natural sweetness, this sorbet makes a perfect guilt-free treat for a hot summer day.

Prep Time: 5 minutes

Ingredients (serves 1):

- 1 cup frozen mixed berries (strawberries, blueberries, raspberries, blackberries)
- ¼ cup water
- 1 tbsp honey (optional)
- Lime juice (optional)
- Fresh mint leaves for garnish (optional)

Instructions:

1. Combine frozen berries and water in your Ninja Creami.
2. Process according to manufacturer's instructions until smooth and sorbet-like.
3. Taste and adjust sweetness with honey, if desired. Add a squeeze of lime juice for a brighter flavor (optional).
4. Serve immediately for a soft-serve consistency, or freeze for 1-2 hours for a firmer sorbet.
5. Garnish with fresh mint leaves for an extra touch of summer (optional).

Nutrition (per serving):

- Calories: 120
- Protein: 1g
- Carbs: 30g
- Fat: 1g

Tips:

- Use any combination of berries you like, such as mango, pineapple, or cherries.
- Adjust the amount of honey to your desired sweetness level.
- For a smoother sorbet, thaw the berries slightly before processing.
- Add a pinch of ginger or chia seeds for an extra boost of flavor and nutrients.
- Drizzle with a squeeze of agave nectar or maple syrup for added sweetness.
- Top with fresh fruit slices, chopped nuts, or a dollop of Greek yogurt for a more decadent treat.

Blood Orange & Prosecco Sorbet: Sparkling Citrus Delight

Elevate your taste buds with this elegant and refreshing blood orange & prosecco sorbet. The vibrant blood orange flavor marries beautifully with the bubbly effervescence of prosecco, creating a light and sophisticated frozen treat perfect for special occasions or a delightful afternoon pick-me-up.

Prep Time: 5 minutes

Ingredients (serves 1):

- 1 cup frozen blood orange segments
- ¼ cup chilled prosecco
- 1 tbsp water (optional)
- 1 tsp powdered sugar or honey (optional)
- Fresh blood orange slice for garnish (optional)

Instructions:

1. Combine frozen blood orange segments and prosecco in your Ninja Creami.
2. Process according to manufacturer's instructions until smooth and sorbet-like.
3. If the mixture seems too thick, add a tablespoon of water at a time until desired consistency is reached.
4. Taste and adjust sweetness with powdered sugar or honey, if desired.
5. Serve immediately for a soft-serve consistency, or freeze for 1-2 hours for a firmer sorbet.

6. Garnish with a fresh blood orange slice for an extra touch of elegance (optional).

Nutrition (per serving):

- Calories: 150 (approximate, may vary depending on prosecco)
- Protein: 1g
- Carbs: 20g
- Fat: 0g

Tips:

- Use freshly squeezed blood orange juice instead of frozen segments for a brighter citrus flavor. Freeze the juice in an ice cube tray before processing.
- If you don't have prosecco, substitute with another lightly sparkling white wine or club soda.
- For a richer flavor, add a drizzle of blood orange liqueur before processing.
- Decorate with a sprig of mint or edible flowers for a festive touch.
- Serve alongside biscotti cookies or dark chocolate shavings for a decadent pairing.

Mango & Chili Sorbet: A Sweet & Spicy Adventure

This vibrant mango & chili sorbet is a captivating dance of sweet and spicy flavors! Juicy mango bursts with sweetness, balanced by the subtle heat of chili pepper, creating a refreshingly unique and unforgettable frozen treat.

Prep Time: 5 minutes

Ingredients (serves 1):

- 1 cup frozen mango chunks
- ¼ cup unsweetened coconut milk
- 1 tbsp lime juice
- 1/2 tsp finely chopped red chili pepper (adjust to your spice preference)
- 1 tsp honey (optional)
- Fresh mint leaves for garnish (optional)

Instructions:

1. Combine frozen mango chunks, coconut milk, lime juice, and chili pepper in your Ninja Creami.
2. Process according to manufacturer's instructions until smooth and sorbet-like.
3. Taste and adjust sweetness with honey, if desired. Start with a smaller amount and gradually add more to taste.
4. Serve immediately for a soft-serve consistency, or freeze for 1-2 hours for a firmer sorbet.
5. Garnish with fresh mint leaves for an extra touch of freshness (optional).

Nutrition (per serving):

- Calories: 180 (approximate, may vary depending on sweetness)
- Protein: 1g
- Carbs: 40g
- Fat: 5g

Tips:

- Use different types of chili peppers for varying spice levels. Start with milder options like Fresno or jalapeño, and adjust according to your tolerance.
- If you don't have fresh chili pepper, substitute with ¼ tsp chili powder or a few drops of hot sauce.
- Substitute frozen pineapple for some of the mango for a tropical twist.
- Add a pinch of ginger or a squeeze of orange juice for additional depth of flavor.
- Drizzle with a touch of agave nectar or maple syrup for an extra touch of sweetness.
- Top with chopped nuts, toasted coconut flakes, or fresh berries for added texture and flavor.

Watermelon & Cucumber Sorbet: Cool & Hydrating Delight

Escape the heat with this refreshingly light and hydrating watermelon & cucumber sorbet. Sweet, juicy watermelon pairs perfectly with the cool, crisp cucumber, creating a delicious and nutritious frozen treat perfect for any summer day.

Prep Time: 5 minutes

Ingredients (serves 1):

- 1 cup frozen seedless watermelon chunks
- ½ cup frozen cucumber chunks
- ¼ cup water (optional)
- 1 tbsp lime juice (optional)
- Fresh mint leaves for garnish (optional)

Instructions:

1. Combine frozen watermelon and cucumber chunks in your Ninja Creami.
2. Process according to manufacturer's instructions until smooth and sorbet-like.
3. If the mixture seems too thick, add a tablespoon of water at a time until desired consistency is reached.
4. Taste and adjust sweetness with lime juice, if desired. Start with a small amount and gradually add more to taste.
5. Serve immediately for a soft-serve consistency, or freeze for 1-2 hours for a firmer sorbet.
6. Garnish with fresh mint leaves for an extra touch of freshness (optional).

Nutrition (per serving):

- Calories: 80 (approximate)
- Protein: 1g
- Carbs: 20g
- Fat: 0g

Tips:

- Use ripe watermelon for maximum sweetness and flavor.
- If you don't have frozen cucumbers, you can use fresh cucumbers. Just peel and chop it into small pieces before freezing for at least 2 hours.
- For a richer flavor, add a drizzle of honey or agave nectar before processing.
- Substitute frozen cantaloupe or honeydew for some of the watermelon for a different melon twist.
- Add a pinch of ginger or a squeeze of orange juice for an extra punch of flavor.
- Drizzle with a touch of balsamic glaze or lime zest for a unique flavor addition.
- Top with fresh berries, chopped nuts, or a dollop of Greek yogurt for added texture and protein.

Pineapple & Mint Sorbet: Tropical Escape in a Bowl

Immerse yourself in island vibes with this vibrant pineapple & mint sorbet! Bursting with juicy pineapple sweetness and infused with refreshing mint notes, this is a perfect frozen treat for any day, offering a taste of the tropics in every bite.

Prep Time: 5 minutes

Ingredients (serves 1):

- 1 cup frozen pineapple chunks
- ¼ cup unsweetened coconut milk
- 1 tbsp lime juice
- 10-15 fresh mint leaves
- 1 tsp honey (optional)
- Fresh mint sprig for garnish (optional)

Instructions:

1. Combine frozen pineapple chunks, coconut milk, lime juice, and mint leaves in your Ninja Creami.
2. Process according to manufacturer's instructions until smooth and sorbet-like.
3. Taste and adjust sweetness with honey, if desired. Start with a smaller amount and gradually add more to taste.
4. Serve immediately for a soft-serve consistency, or freeze for 1-2 hours for a firmer sorbet.
5. Garnish with a fresh mint sprig for an extra touch of freshness (optional).

Nutrition (per serving):
- Calories: 200 (approximate)
- Protein: 1g
- Carbs: 40g
- Fat: 5g

Tips:

- Use fresh or frozen pineapple, whichever you have on hand. If using fresh, freeze the chunks for at least 2 hours before processing.
- Substitute frozen mango or banana for some of the pineapple for a different tropical twist.
- Experiment with different types of mint, such as spearmint or peppermint, for varying flavor profiles.
- Add a pinch of ginger or a squeeze of orange juice for an extra layer of flavor.
- Drizzle with a touch of agave nectar or maple syrup for an extra touch of sweetness.
- Top with chopped nuts, toasted coconut flakes, or fresh berries for added texture and flavor.

Raspberry & Rose Sorbet: A Delicate Floral Delight

Indulge in a sophisticated and refreshing treat with this raspberry & rose sorbet. Juicy raspberries meld beautifully with the floral essence of rosewater, creating a delicate and unique frozen treat perfect for special occasions or a delightful afternoon pick-me-up.

Prep Time: 5 minutes

Ingredients (serves 1):

- 1 cup frozen raspberries
- ¼ cup water
- 1 tbsp honey (optional)
- 1 tsp rosewater
- Fresh mint sprig for garnish (optional)

Instructions:

1. Combine frozen raspberries and water in your Ninja Creami.
2. Process according to manufacturer's instructions until smooth and sorbet-like.
3. Taste and adjust sweetness with honey, if desired. Start with a small amount and gradually add more to taste.
4. Stir in the rosewater gently, ensuring it's evenly incorporated.
5. Serve immediately for a soft-serve consistency, or freeze for 1-2 hours for a firmer sorbet.

6. Garnish with a fresh mint sprig for an extra touch of elegance (optional).

Nutrition (per serving):

- Calories: 120 (approximate, may vary depending on sweetness)
- Protein: 1g
- Carbs: 30g
- Fat: 1g

Tips:

- Use fresh raspberries if you prefer, but frozen ones will create a thicker sorbet.
- Substitute frozen blueberries or strawberries for some of the raspberries for a different berry flavor.
- For a richer flavor, add a few drops of rose oil instead of rosewater.
- Drizzle with a touch of agave nectar or maple syrup for an extra touch of sweetness.
- Top with chopped nuts, edible flowers, or a dollop of whipped cream for a more decadent treat.

Blackberry & Balsamic Sorbet: Sweet & Tangy Perfection

Dive into a symphony of sweet and tangy flavors with this blackberry & balsamic sorbet! Bursting with juicy blackberry sweetness, balanced by the subtle balsamic vinegar reduction, this sorbet offers a complex and refreshing frozen treat perfect for any summer day.

Prep Time: 5 minutes (plus 15 minutes for balsamic reduction)

Ingredients (serves 1):

- 1 cup frozen blackberries
- ¼ cup water
- 1 tbsp honey (optional)
- 1 tsp balsamic vinegar reduction (store-bought or homemade)
- Fresh mint leaves for garnish (optional)
- Balsamic Reduction (optional):
- ¼ cup balsamic vinegar

Instructions:

For the balsamic reduction (optional):

- In a small saucepan, heat the balsamic vinegar over medium heat until it simmers.
- Reduce heat to low and simmer gently, stirring occasionally, until the vinegar thickens and reduces by half, about 10-15 minutes. It should coat the back of a spoon without running.
- Set aside to cool completely.

For the sorbet:

- Combine frozen blackberries and water in your Ninja Creami.
- Process according to manufacturer's instructions until smooth and sorbet-like.
- Taste and adjust sweetness with honey, if desired. Start with a smaller amount and gradually add more to taste.
- Gently stir in the balsamic vinegar reduction, ensuring it's evenly incorporated.
- Serve immediately for a soft-serve consistency, or freeze for 1-2 hours for a firmer sorbet.
- Garnish with fresh mint leaves for an extra touch of freshness (optional).

Nutrition (per serving):

- Calories: 130 (approximate, may vary depending on sweetness)
- Protein: 1g, Carbs: 30g, Fat: 1g

Tips:

- Use fresh blackberries if you prefer, but frozen ones will create a thicker sorbet.
- Substitute frozen blueberries or raspberries for some of the blackberries for a different berry flavor.
- Adjust the amount of balsamic reduction to your preference. Start with a little and add more for a stronger tangy flavor.
- Drizzle with a touch of agave nectar or maple syrup for an extra touch of sweetness.
- Top with chopped nuts, toasted coconut flakes, or a dollop of Greek yogurt for added texture and protein..

Lime & Basil Sorbet: A Zesty & Aromatic Delight

This vibrant lime & basil sorbet is a burst of freshness and flavor! The bright acidity of lime is perfectly complemented by the sweet and subtly peppery notes of basil, creating a light and invigorating frozen treat perfect for any day.

Prep Time: 5 minutes

Ingredients (serves 1):

- 1 cup frozen pineapple chunks (peeled and chopped)
- ¼ cup unsweetened coconut milk
- 1 tbsp lime juice
- 10-15 fresh basil leaves
- 1 tsp honey (optional)
- Fresh basil sprig for garnish (optional)

Instructions:

1. Combine frozen pineapple chunks, coconut milk, lime juice, and basil leaves in your Ninja Creami.
2. Process according to manufacturer's instructions until smooth and sorbet-like.
3. Taste and adjust sweetness with honey, if desired. Start with a smaller amount and gradually add more to taste.
4. Serve immediately for a soft-serve consistency, or freeze for 1-2 hours for a firmer sorbet.
5. Garnish with a fresh basil sprig for an extra touch of aroma (optional).

Nutrition (per serving):

- Calories: 200 (approximate)
- Protein: 1g, Carbs: 40g
- Fat: 5g

Tips:

- Substitute frozen mango or banana for some of the pineapple for a different tropical twist.
- Experiment with different types of basil, such as Thai basil or lemon basil, for varying flavor profiles.
- Add a pinch of ginger or a squeeze of orange juice for an extra punch of flavor.
- Drizzle with a touch of agave nectar or maple syrup for an extra touch of sweetness.
- Top with chopped nuts, toasted coconut flakes, or fresh berries for added texture and flavor.

Additional Notes:

1. For a more intense basil flavor, you can blanch the leaves briefly before adding them to the sorbet mixture. Simply dip them in boiling water for 10 seconds, then transfer them to an ice bath to stop the cooking.
2. If you don't have fresh basil, you can use 1/4 teaspoon of dried basil, but the flavor will be less vibrant.
3. Feel free to adjust the amount of lime juice to your preference for a more or less tart sorbet.
4. This lime & basil sorbet recipe is a delicious and refreshing way to enjoy the taste of summer. The combination of sweet and savory flavors is sure to please your palate. Feel free to experiment with different variations and enjoy!

Grapefruit & Elderflower Sorbet: A Sophisticated Citrus Duet

This vibrant grapefruit & elderflower sorbet offers a sophisticated dance of sweet and floral flavors, creating a refreshingly unique frozen treat. The bright acidity of grapefruit blends beautifully with the delicate elderflower notes, leaving your taste buds dancing with delight.

Prep Time: 5 minutes

Ingredients (serves 1):

- 1 cup frozen pink grapefruit segments (peeled and chopped)
- ¼ cup water
- 1-2 tbsp honey (adjust to your taste)
- 1 tbsp elderflower liqueur or cordial
- Fresh mint sprig for garnish (optional)

Instructions:

1. Combine frozen grapefruit segments, water, honey, and elderflower liqueur in your Ninja Creami.
2. Process according to manufacturer's instructions until smooth and sorbet-like.
3. Taste and adjust sweetness with additional honey, if desired. Remember, grapefruit can be naturally quite tart, so adjust to your preference.
4. Serve immediately for a soft-serve consistency, or freeze for 1-2 hours for a firmer sorbet.
5. Garnish with a fresh mint sprig for an extra touch of freshness (optional).

Nutrition (per serving):

- Calories: 150 (approximate, may vary depending on sweetness)
- Protein: 1g
- Carbs: 30g
- Fat: 0g

Tips:

- Substitute frozen blood oranges for some of the grapefruit for a different citrus twist.
- Add a pinch of ginger or a squeeze of lime juice for an extra zing.
- Drizzle with a touch of agave nectar or maple syrup for an alternative sweetener.
- Top with chopped nuts, edible flowers, or a dollop of Greek yogurt for added texture and protein.

Additional Notes:

1. You can substitute non-alcoholic elderflower cordial for the liqueur if you prefer.
2. If you don't have frozen grapefruit segments, you can use fresh grapefruit. Simply peel and chop the flesh, removing as much white pith as possible, and freeze for at least 2 hours before using.
3. For a richer flavor, use a combination of pink grapefruit and ruby red grapefruit.

Pomegranate & Ginger Sorbet: A Burst of Sweet & Spicy Delight

This vibrant pomegranate & ginger sorbet is an explosion of sweet and spicy flavors, offering a refreshingly complex frozen treat. The juicy sweetness of pomegranate perfectly complements the warm bite of ginger, creating a unique and unforgettable taste experience.

Prep Time: 5 minutes

Ingredients (serves 1):

- 1 cup frozen pomegranate arils
- ¼ cup water
- 1 tbsp honey (optional)
- 1 tbsp fresh ginger, finely grated
- Fresh mint sprig for garnish (optional)

Instructions:

1. Combine frozen pomegranate arils, water, honey (if using), and grated ginger in your Ninja Creami.
2. Process according to manufacturer's instructions until smooth and sorbet-like.
3. Taste and adjust sweetness with honey, if desired. Start with a smaller amount and gradually add more to taste.
4. Serve immediately for a soft-serve consistency, or freeze for 1-2 hours for a firmer sorbet.
5. Garnish with a fresh mint sprig for an extra touch of freshness (optional).

Nutrition (per serving):
- Calories: 170 (approximate, may vary depending on sweetness)
- Protein: 1g
- Carbs: 40g
- Fat: 0g

Tips:

- If you don't have fresh ginger, you can use 1/4 teaspoon of ground ginger, but the flavor will be less intense.
- Substitute frozen raspberries or strawberries for some of the pomegranate arils for a different berry twist.
- Add a squeeze of lime juice for an extra touch of brightness.
- Drizzle with a touch of agave nectar or maple syrup for an alternative sweetener.
- Top with chopped nuts, toasted coconut flakes, or a dollop of Greek yogurt for added texture and protein.

Additional Notes:

- You can find frozen pomegranate arils in most grocery stores or online.
- If you want a smoother sorbet, you can strain the mixture through a fine-mesh sieve after processing.
- Feel free to adjust the amount of ginger to your spice preference. Start with a little and add more to taste.

Sun-Kissed Strawberry & Basil Sorbet

This vibrant sorbet captures the essence of summer with its juicy strawberries and fresh basil notes. Perfect for a refreshing treat or a light dessert, it's simple to make and bursting with flavor.

Prep Time: 5 minutes

Ingredients (serves 1):

- 1 cup frozen strawberries (hulled and sliced)
- ¼ cup water
- 1 tbsp honey (optional)
- 5-7 fresh basil leaves
- Squeeze of fresh lemon juice (optional)
- Fresh basil sprig for garnish (optional)

Instructions:

1. Combine the frozen strawberries, water, honey (if using), and basil leaves in your Ninja Creami.
2. Process according to manufacturer's instructions until smooth and sorbet-like.
3. Taste and adjust sweetness with additional honey, if desired.
4. Add a squeeze of lemon juice for a brighter flavor (optional).
5. Serve immediately for a soft-serve consistency, or freeze for 1-2 hours for a firmer sorbet.
6. Garnish with a fresh basil sprig for an extra touch of summer (optional).

Nutrition (per serving):

- Calories: 120 (approximate, may vary depending on sweetness)
- Protein: 1g
- Carbs: 30g
- Fat: 1g

Tips:

- Use ripe, sweet strawberries for the best flavor.
- Freeze the strawberries for at least 2 hours before using for a thicker sorbet.
- Substitute frozen raspberries or blueberries for some of the strawberries for a different berry twist.
- For a richer flavor, use a few drops of almond extract instead of honey.
- Drizzle with a touch of balsamic vinegar reduction for a sweet and tangy twist.
- Top with chopped nuts, fresh mint leaves, or a dollop of whipped cream for added texture and flavor.

Yogurt Bowls

Chocolate Chia Seed Yogurt Bowl:

A Deliciously Nutritious Start to Your Day

This chocolate chia seed yogurt bowl is the perfect blend of indulgence and healthy nutrients, making it a satisfying and delicious breakfast or snack. Packed with protein, fiber, and antioxidants, it's a guilt-free way to satisfy your sweet tooth while nourishing your body.

Ingredients (serves 1):

- 1/2 cup plain Greek yogurt (or your preferred yogurt)
- 1/4 cup unsweetened almond milk (or your preferred milk)
- 2 tbsp chia seeds
- 1 tbsp unsweetened cocoa powder
- 1/4 tsp ground cinnamon
- 1/4 cup fresh or frozen berries (your choice)
- 1/4 cup sliced banana or other fruit (optional)
- Handful of chopped nuts or seeds (optional)
- Drizzle of honey or maple syrup (optional)

Nutritional Information (approximate per serving):

- Calories: 350
- Protein: 20g
- Carbs: 30g
- Fat: 15g

Instructions:

1. In a small bowl, whisk together yogurt, almond milk, chia seeds, cocoa powder, and cinnamon until well combined.
2. Cover and refrigerate for at least 30 minutes, or overnight for a thicker consistency.
3. Meanwhile, slice your chosen fruit and chop any nuts or seeds.
4. Once the chia seed mixture has thickened, assemble your bowl by pouring it into a serving dish.
5. Top with your favorite fruits, nuts, and seeds.
6. Drizzle with honey or maple syrup for added sweetness (optional).

Tips:

- For a richer chocolate flavor, use dark cocoa powder or add a tablespoon of chocolate chips to the mixture.
- Swap the berries for other fruits like mango, pineapple, or kiwi for a different flavor profile.
- Boost the protein content with a scoop of protein powder mixed into the yogurt.
- Add a dollop of nut butter for extra creaminess and healthy fats.
- Sprinkle with shredded coconut or granola for a textural contrast.
- Get creative with toppings! Use edible flowers, chia seeds, goji berries, or even a drizzle of dark chocolate for a decadent touch.

Blueberry   Acai   Yogurt   Bowl:

An Antioxidant Powerhouse

This vibrant blueberry acai yogurt bowl is more than just a delicious breakfast – it's a nutritional powerhouse! Packed with antioxidants, healthy fats, and fiber, it's a satisfying way to start your day or enjoy a refreshing snack.

Ingredients (serves 1):

- ½ cup plain Greek yogurt (or your preferred yogurt)
- ¼ cup frozen acai berry puree (unsweetened)
- ¼ cup unsweetened plant-based milk (almond, coconut, oat, etc.)
- ½ cup fresh or frozen blueberries
- ¼ cup granola (optional)
- ¼ cup chopped nuts and seeds (almonds, chia seeds, hemp seeds, etc.)
- 1 tbsp honey or maple syrup (optional)

Nutritional Information (approximate per serving):

- Calories: 300-400 (depending on ingredients)
- Protein: 20g (with protein powder)
- Carbs: 30g
- Fat: 15g

Instructions:

1. In a blender, combine yogurt, acai puree, and milk. Blend until smooth and creamy.
2. Pour the mixture into a bowl.
3. Top with fresh or frozen blueberries.
4. Add granola, nuts, and seeds for extra texture and flavor.
5. Drizzle with honey or maple syrup for added sweetness (optional).

Tips:

- If you don't have frozen acai puree, you can use acai powder (start with 1 teaspoon and adjust to taste).
- Substitute other berries like raspberries, strawberries, or blackberries for blueberries.
- Boost the protein content with a scoop of protein powder mixed into the yogurt.
- Blend in a handful of spinach or kale for a hidden veggie boost.
- Add a dollop of nut butter for extra creaminess and healthy fats.
- Drizzle with chia seeds, goji berries, or shredded coconut for added nutrients and visual appeal.

Tropical Paradise: Mango Coconut Yogurt Bowl

Escape to the tropics with this vibrant and flavorful mango coconut yogurt bowl! Bursting with juicy mango sweetness and creamy coconut richness, it's a satisfying breakfast, snack, or even a light dessert that nourishes your body and tantalize your taste buds.

Ingredients (serves 1):

- 1/2 cup plain Greek yogurt (or your preferred yogurt)
- 1/4 cup unsweetened coconut milk
- 1/4 cup frozen mango chunks
- 1/2 mango, sliced or diced (fresh or frozen)
- 1 tablespoon shredded unsweetened coconut
- 1 tablespoon chopped walnuts or pecans (optional)
- 1 tablespoon hemp seeds or chia seeds (optional)
- Drizzle of honey or maple syrup (optional)

Nutritional Information (approximate per serving):

- Calories: 350-400 (depending on ingredients)
- Protein: 20g (with protein powder)
- Carbs: 30g
- Fat: 15g

Instructions:

1. In a blender, combine yogurt, coconut milk, and frozen mango chunks. Blend until smooth and creamy.
2. Pour the mixture into a bowl.
3. Top with fresh or frozen mango slices/dices.
4. Sprinkle with shredded coconut, chopped nuts, and hemp/chia seeds for added texture and flavor.
5. Drizzle with honey or maple syrup for extra sweetness (optional).

Tips:

- Substitute frozen pineapple or papaya for some of the mango for a different tropical twist.
- Add a squeeze of lime juice for a touch of brightness.
- Boost the protein content with a scoop of protein powder mixed into the yogurt.
- Blend in a handful of spinach or kale for a hidden veggie boost.
- Top with granola, granola clusters, or muesli for an extra crunch.
- Drizzle with melted dark chocolate or tahini for a decadent touch.
- Get creative with toppings! Use edible flowers, goji berries, or even a dusting of matcha powder for a unique flavor and visual appeal.

Classic Comfort: Banana Walnut Yogurt Bowl

This timeless combination of banana, walnut, and yogurt is a breakfast or snack staple for a reason! It's simple, satisfying, and packed with nutrients, making it the perfect base for endless customization.

Ingredients (serves 1):

- 1/2 cup plain Greek yogurt (or your preferred yogurt)
- 1/4 cup granola (optional)
- 1/2 banana, sliced
- 1/4 cup chopped walnuts
- 1 tablespoon honey or maple syrup (optional)
- Pinch of cinnamon (optional)
- Fresh mint sprig for garnish (optional)

Nutritional Information (approximate per serving):

- Calories: 300-400 (depending on ingredients)
- Protein: 20g (with protein powder)
- Carbs: 30g
- Fat: 15g

Instructions:

1. In a bowl, layer the yogurt and granola (if using).
2. Top with sliced banana and chopped walnuts.
3. Drizzle with honey or maple syrup for added sweetness (optional).
4. Sprinkle with cinnamon for a warm spice touch (optional).

5. Garnish with a fresh mint sprig for a pop of color (optional).

Tips:

- Substitute other fruits like berries, mango, or pineapple for bananas.
- Use different types of nuts like almonds, pecans, or even a nut butter drizzle.
- Add a dollop of chia seeds or hemp seeds for extra protein and omega-3s.
- Blend in a handful of spinach or kale for a hidden veggie boost.
- Top with dried fruits, coconut flakes, or a sprinkle of dark chocolate chips for added flavor and texture.
- Drizzle with tahini, nut butter, or even melted dark chocolate for a richer flavor profile.
- Get creative with spices! Consider a pinch of ginger, cardamom, or nutmeg for a unique twist.

Raspberry Almond Symphony: A Sweet & Nutty Delight

Dive into a symphony of textures and flavors with this vibrant raspberry almond yogurt bowl! Sweet and juicy raspberries meld perfectly with creamy yogurt and crunchy almonds, creating a satisfying and delicious breakfast, snack, or even dessert.

Ingredients (serves 1):

- ½ cup plain Greek yogurt (or your preferred yogurt)
- ¼ cup fresh or frozen raspberries
- ¼ cup granola (optional)
- ¼ cup sliced almonds
- 1 tablespoon almond butter (optional)
- 1 tablespoon chia seeds (optional)
- Drizzle of honey or maple syrup (optional)
- Fresh mint sprig for garnish (optional)

Nutritional Information (approximate per serving):

- Calories: 300-400 (depending on ingredients)
- Protein: 20g (with protein powder)
- Carbs: 30g
- Fat: 15g

Instructions:

1. In a bowl, layer the yogurt and granola (if using).
2. Top with fresh or frozen raspberries.
3. Sprinkle with sliced almonds and chia seeds (if using).
4. Drizzle with almond butter for a nutty richness (optional).
5. Add a touch of honey or maple syrup for extra sweetness (optional).
6. Garnish with a fresh mint sprig for a pop of color (optional).

Tips:

- Substitute other berries like blueberries, strawberries, or blackberries for raspberries.
- Use different types of nuts like pecans, walnuts, or even a sprinkle of sunflower seeds.
- For a thicker consistency, blend some of the raspberries with a tablespoon of yogurt before layering.
- Add a dollop of mashed banana or avocado for extra creaminess and healthy fats.
- Incorporate a scoop of protein powder for an added protein boost.
- Drizzle with melted dark chocolate, tahini, or even a touch of balsamic glaze for a unique flavor twist.
- Get creative with spices! Consider a pinch of cinnamon, cardamom, or ginger for a warm touch.

Decadent Delight: Dark Chocolate Avocado Yogurt Bowl

This luxurious dark chocolate avocado yogurt bowl offers a surprisingly healthy and satisfying treat. Creamy avocado and rich dark chocolate combine beautifully with the tang of yogurt, creating a flavor explosion that's perfect for satisfying your sweet tooth without guilt.

Ingredients (serves 1):

- 1/2 cup plain Greek yogurt (or your preferred yogurt)
- 1/4 cup unsweetened almond milk (or your preferred milk)
- 1/4 medium avocado, ripe and peeled
- 1 tablespoon unsweetened cocoa powder
- 1 tablespoon honey or maple syrup (optional)
- Pinch of sea salt
- 1/4 cup granola (optional)
- 1/4 cup fresh berries (optional)
- 1/4 cup chopped nuts (optional)
- 1 tablespoon dark chocolate shavings (optional)

Nutritional Information (approximate per serving):

- Calories: 350-450 (depending on ingredients)
- Protein: 20g (with protein powder)
- Carbs: 30g
- Fat: 20g

Instructions:

1. In a blender, combine yogurt, almond milk, avocado, cocoa powder, honey (if using), and sea salt. Blend until smooth and creamy.
2. Pour the mixture into a bowl.
3. Top with granola, berries, nuts, and/or dark chocolate shavings, as desired.

Tips:

- Substitute frozen bananas for some of the avocado for a thicker and creamier base.
- Use coconut milk instead of almond milk for a richer flavor.
- If you don't have cocoa powder, you can use 2 tablespoons of melted dark chocolate, but adjust the sweetness accordingly.
- Add a scoop of protein powder for an extra protein boost.
- Spice it up with a pinch of cayenne pepper or cinnamon.
- Drizzle with chia seeds, hemp seeds, or goji berries for added nutrients and texture.
- Get creative with toppings! Experiment with different fruits, nuts, seeds, and even a dollop of nut butter for a personalized touch.

Zesty & Bright: Lemon Poppy Seed Yogurt Bowl

This light and refreshing lemon poppy seed yogurt bowl is a sunshine-filled treat perfect for breakfast, a snack, or even dessert. The vibrant citrus notes of lemon dance with the sweet and crunchy poppy seeds, creating a delightful flavor combination that's both nourishing and delicious.

Ingredients (serves 1):

- ½ cup plain Greek yogurt (or your preferred yogurt)
- ¼ cup unsweetened almond milk (or your preferred milk)
- 2 tbsp fresh lemon juice
- 1 tbsp honey or maple syrup (optional)
- 1 tbsp chia seeds (optional)
- 2 tbsp poppy seeds
- ¼ cup fresh or frozen berries (optional)
- ¼ cup granola (optional)
- Fresh mint sprig for garnish (optional)

Nutritional Information (approximate per serving):

- Calories: 250-350 (depending on ingredients)
- Protein: 20g (with protein powder)
- Carbs: 30g
- Fat: 10g

Instructions:

- In a bowl, whisk together yogurt, almond milk, lemon juice, and honey (if using).
- Divide the mixture evenly between two small bowls or one larger bowl.

- Sprinkle one half with chia seeds and the other half with poppy seeds.
- Top with fresh or frozen berries and granola, as desired.
- Garnish with a fresh mint sprig for a touch of color (optional).

Tips:

- Substitute other citrus fruits like grapefruit or orange for lemon for a different twist.
- Use a combination of chia seeds and poppy seeds for a more textured topping.
- Add a dollop of nut butter for extra creaminess and healthy fats.
- Incorporate a scoop of protein powder for an added protein boost.
- Drizzle with chia seeds, hemp seeds, or goji berries for added nutrients and visual appeal.
- Get creative with spices! Consider a pinch of ginger, turmeric, or cardamom for a unique flavor profile.

Classic Delight: Strawberry Granola Yogurt Bowl

This timeless combination of strawberries, granola, and yogurt is a breakfast or snack staple for a reason! It's simple, satisfying, and packed with flavor and nutrients, making it the perfect base for endless customization.

Ingredients (serves 1):

- 1/2 cup plain Greek yogurt (or your preferred yogurt)
- 1/4 cup granola (optional)
- 1/2 cup fresh or frozen strawberries, sliced
- 1 tablespoon honey or maple syrup (optional)
- Fresh mint sprig for garnish (optional)

Nutritional Information (approximate per serving):

- Calories: 300-400 (depending on ingredients)
- Protein: 20g (with protein powder)
- Carbs: 30g
- Fat: 15g

Instructions:

1. In a bowl, layer the yogurt and granola (if using).
2. Top with sliced strawberries.
3. Drizzle with honey or maple syrup for added sweetness (optional).
4. Garnish with a fresh mint sprig for a pop of color (optional).

Tips:

- Substitute other fruits like blueberries, mango, or pineapple for strawberries.
- Use different types of granola for a textural variation, like clusters, muesli, or even homemade granola.
- Add a dollop of chia seeds or hemp seeds for extra protein and omega-3s.
- Blend in a handful of spinach or kale for a hidden veggie boost.
- Top with dried fruits, coconut flakes, or a sprinkle of dark chocolate chips for added flavor and texture.
- Drizzle with tahini, nut butter, or even melted dark chocolate for a richer flavor profile.
- Get creative with spices! Consider a pinch of cinnamon, cardamom, or nutmeg for a warm touch.

Here are some additional variations you can explore:

Strawberry Shortcake Bowl: Add a dollop of whipped cream and crumbled shortbread cookies for a decadent twist.

Tropical Fiesta: Combine strawberries with mango, pineapple, and toasted coconut flakes for a burst of island vibes.

Green Powerhouse: Blend a handful of spinach or kale into the yogurt for a hidden veggie boost, and top with chia seeds and hemp seeds for extra protein and nutrients.

Spiced Delight: Add a pinch of cinnamon, cardamom, or ginger to the yogurt for a warm and flavorful twist.

Classic Combo: Peanut Butter Banana Yogurt Bowl

This timeless combination of peanut butter, banana, and yogurt is a fan-favorite for its simplicity, satisfaction, and delightful flavor profile. It's also incredibly versatile, allowing for endless customization to suit your taste and dietary needs.

Ingredients (serves 1):

- ½ cup plain Greek yogurt (or your preferred yogurt)
- ¼ cup granola (optional)
- ½ banana, sliced or mashed
- 1-2 tablespoons peanut butter (smooth or chunky, your choice)
- Drizzle of honey or maple syrup (optional)
- Pinch of cinnamon (optional)
- Crushed peanuts or chopped nuts for garnish (optional)

Nutritional Information (approximate per serving):

- Calories: 300-400 (depending on ingredients)
- Protein: 20g (with protein powder)
- Carbs: 30g
- Fat: 15g

Instructions:

1. In a bowl, layer the yogurt and granola (if using).
2. Top with sliced or mashed banana.
3. Drizzle with your desired amount of peanut butter.
4. For added sweetness, drizzle with honey or maple syrup (optional).
5. Sprinkle with a pinch of cinnamon for a warm touch (optional).
6. Garnish with crushed peanuts or chopped nuts for extra texture and flavor (optional).

Tips:

- Substitute other fruits like berries, mango, or pineapple for bananas.
- Use different types of nut butter like almond butter, cashew butter, or even sunflower seed butter for variety.
- Add a dollop of chia seeds or hemp seeds for extra protein and omega-3s.
- Blend in a handful of spinach or kale for a hidden veggie boost.
- Top with dried fruits, coconut flakes, or a sprinkle of dark chocolate chips for additional flavor and texture.
- Drizzle with tahini, melted dark chocolate, or even a touch of balsamic glaze for a unique flavor twist.
- Get creative with spices! Consider a pinch of ginger, cardamom, or even a dash of cayenne pepper for a spicy kick.

Here are some additional variations you can explore:

Chocolate Dream: Mix a tablespoon of cocoa powder into the yogurt for a rich chocolatey base.

Protein Powerhouse: Add a scoop of protein powder to the yogurt for an extra protein boost.
Tropical Paradise: Top with diced mango, pineapple, and toasted coconut flakes for a tropical twist.

Green Machine: Blend a handful of spinach or kale into the yogurt for a hidden veggie boost, and top with chia seeds and hemp seeds for extra protein and nutrients.

Pumpkin Spice Yogurt Bowl:

Ingredients (serves 1):

- ½ cup plain Greek yogurt (or your preferred yogurt)
- ¼ cup unsweetened almond milk (or your preferred milk)
- ¼ cup unsweetened pumpkin puree
- 1 tablespoon honey or maple syrup (optional)
- ½ teaspoon ground cinnamon
- ¼ teaspoon ground ginger
- ¼ teaspoon ground nutmeg
- Pinch of ground cloves
- ¼ cup granola (optional)
- ¼ cup fresh or frozen berries (optional)
- Chopped nuts and seeds (optional)
- Drizzle of tahini or nut butter (optional)

Instructions:

1. In a bowl, whisk together yogurt, almond milk, pumpkin puree, honey (if using), and spices until well combined.
2. Pour the mixture into a serving bowl.
3. Top with granola, berries, nuts, and seeds, as desired.
4. Drizzle with tahini or nut butter for added richness (optional).

Tips:

- For a thicker consistency, use less almond milk or blend some of the berries with a tablespoon of yogurt before layering.
- Substitute other fall spices like cardamom or allspice for a different flavor profile.
- Add a scoop of protein powder for an extra protein boost.

- Drizzle with chia seeds, hemp seeds, or goji berries for added nutrients and visual appeal.
- Get creative with toppings! Experiment with different fruits, nuts, seeds, and even a dollop of mashed sweet potato for a more fall-inspired treat.

Nutritional Information (approximate per serving):

- Calories: 300-400 (depending on ingredients)
- Protein: 20g (with protein powder)
- Carbs: 30g
- Fat: 15g

Additional Variations:

Chocolate Chip Surprise: Fold in dark chocolate chips or mini dark chocolate bars for a decadent treat.

Caramel Crunch: Drizzle with melted coconut oil or tahini mixed with a drop of honey for a caramel-like flavor and add chopped pecans or almonds for an added crunch.

Maple Pecan: Use maple syrup as your sweetener and top with chopped pecans and a sprinkle of pumpkin seeds for a nutty and sweet combination.

Spiced Pear: Top with diced pears that have been sautéed with a touch of butter, cinnamon, and nutmeg for a warm and comforting finish.

Smoothie Bowls

Island Escape in a Bowl: Creamy Pineapple Coconut Smoothie Bowl

Escape to paradise with this vibrant Pineapple Coconut Smoothie Bowl! Creamy, dreamy, and naturally sweetened, it's a taste of the tropics that's both refreshing and nutritious. Packed with sunshine yellow and island vibes, this smoothie bowl is the perfect way to start your day, enjoy a guilt-free snack, or cool down on a hot afternoon.

Ingredients (serves 1):

- 1 cup frozen pineapple chunks
- 1/2 frozen banana
- 1/4 cup unsweetened coconut milk
- 1/4 cup water
- 1 tablespoon shredded unsweetened coconut (optional)
- 1/4 teaspoon ground cinnamon (optional)
- Fresh pineapple slices and shredded coconut for topping

Instructions:

1. Blend the frozen pineapple chunks, banana, coconut milk, and water in a blender until smooth and creamy.
2. Taste and adjust the sweetness or consistency as desired. Add more frozen banana or coconut milk for thickness, or a splash of water for a thinner consistency.
3. Pour the smoothie mixture into a bowl.

4. Top with your favorite island-inspired toppings! Some ideas include fresh pineapple slices, shredded coconut, toasted nuts, granola, chia seeds, or even a drizzle of melted dark chocolate.
5. Enjoy your tropical escape in a bowl!

Nutritional Information (per serving):

- Calories: 250-300 (depending on toppings)
- Protein: 2g
- Carbs: 50g
- Fat: 10g

Tips & Variations:

- Boost the protein: Add a scoop of protein powder to the blend for an extra protein kick.
- Make it creamier: Use full-fat coconut milk for a richer taste and texture.
- Berry twist: Swap out some of the pineapple for frozen berries like strawberries or mango for a different flavor combination.
- Green power: Add a handful of spinach or kale to the blend for a hidden veggie boost.
- Spice it up: Add a pinch of ginger, turmeric, or cardamom for a warm and flavorful twist.
- Get creative: Have fun experimenting with different toppings and mix-ins to personalize your smoothie bowl!

Sunset Bliss: Blueberry Mango Smoothie Bowl

Dive into a vibrant medley of sweet & tart with this Blueberry Mango Smoothie Bowl! Bursting with juicy blueberries, sunshine-kissed mango, and creamy coconut milk, it's an explosion of flavor and color that nourishes your body and tantalize your taste buds. Perfect for breakfast, a refreshing snack, or a healthy dessert, this smoothie bowl is a tropical escape in every spoonful.

Ingredients (serves 1):

- 1 cup frozen blueberries
- 1/2 cup frozen mango chunks
- 1/2 frozen banana
- 1/4 cup unsweetened coconut milk
- 1/4 cup plain Greek yogurt (optional)
- 1/4 teaspoon ground ginger (optional)
- Fresh blueberries, mango slices, and granola for topping

Instructions:

1. In a blender, combine the frozen blueberries, mango chunks, banana, coconut milk, and Greek yogurt (if using).
2. Blend until smooth and creamy, adjusting the consistency by adding more coconut milk for a thinner texture or frozen banana for thicker.
3. Taste and add the ginger, if desired, for a warm kick.
4. Pour the smoothie mixture into a bowl.
5. Get creative with your toppings! Arrange fresh blueberries, mango slices, and granola for a visually-appealing and textural contrast.

Nutritional Information (per serving):

- Calories: 300-350 (depending on ingredients)
- Protein: 10g (with Greek yogurt)
- Carbs: 50g
- Fat: 15g

Tips & Variations:

- Boost the protein: Add a scoop of protein powder for an extra protein boost.
- Make it sweeter: Drizzle with honey, maple syrup, or agave nectar for added sweetness.
- Berry blend: Swap some blueberries for other berries like raspberries or strawberries for a different flavor profile.
- Green power: Add a handful of spinach or kale to the blend for a hidden veggie boost.
- Spice it up: Add a pinch of cinnamon, cardamom, or turmeric for a warm and flavorful twist.
- Decadent twist: Drizzle with melted dark chocolate or tahini for a rich and indulgent touch.
- Get creative: Explore different toppings like chia seeds, nuts, shredded coconut, or even edible flowers for added flavor and visual appeal.

Pink Delight: Strawberry Banana Smoothie Bowl

Get ready for a flavor explosion with this Pink Delight: Strawberry Banana Smoothie Bowl! Combining the classic duo of sweet strawberries and creamy bananas, this bowl is a burst of fruity sunshine in every bite. Packed with nutrients and naturally sweetened, it's a guilt-free indulgence that's perfect for breakfast, a snack, or a post-workout treat.

Ingredients (serves 1):

- 1 cup frozen strawberries
- 1/2 frozen banana
- 1/4 cup unsweetened almond milk (or your preferred milk)
- 1/4 cup plain Greek yogurt (optional, for extra protein)
- 1 tablespoon chia seeds (optional, for thickening)
- Fresh strawberries, banana slices, and granola for topping

Instructions:

1. Blend all ingredients in a blender until smooth and creamy. Adjust consistency by adding more milk for thinner or frozen banana for thicker.
2. Taste and adjust sweetness as desired. Honey, maple syrup, or agave nectar are great options.
3. Pour the smoothie mixture into a bowl.
4. Unleash your creativity with toppings! Arrange fresh strawberries, banana slices, and granola for a delightful texture and flavor combination.

Nutritional Information (per serving):

- Calories: 250-300 (depending on ingredients)
- Protein: 5g (with Greek yogurt)
- Carbs: 40g
- Fat: 5g

Tips & Variations:

- Boost the protein: Add a scoop of protein powder for an extra protein kick.
- Tropical twist: Swap some strawberries for frozen pineapple or mango for a vibrant flavor fiesta.
- Berry medley: Use a mix of different berries like raspberries or blueberries for a more complex flavor profile.
- Green power: Add a handful of spinach or kale to the blend for a hidden veggie boost.
- Spice it up: Add a pinch of cinnamon, nutmeg, or ginger for a warm and flavorful twist.
- Decadent touch: Drizzle with melted dark chocolate or nut butter for a rich and indulgent finish.
- Get creative: Explore different toppings like chia seeds, hemp seeds, shredded coconut, or even edible flowers for added flavor and visual appeal.

Green Glow Up: Kale Apple Smoothie Bowl

Embrace the green goddess within with this Green Glow Up: Kale Apple Smoothie Bowl! This vibrant bowl packs a powerful punch of vitamins, minerals, and antioxidants, all while delivering a refreshingly sweet and tart flavor combination. Perfect for those seeking a healthy and delicious breakfast, post-workout pick-me-up, or light lunch, this smoothie bowl is your ticket to a greener you.

Ingredients (serves 1):

- 1 cup baby kale or spinach
- 1/2 green apple, cored and chopped
- 1/2 frozen banana
- 1/4 cup unsweetened almond milk (or your preferred milk)
- 1/4 cup plain Greek yogurt (optional, for extra protein)
- 1 tablespoon chia seeds (optional, for thickening)
- Fresh apple slices, chopped kale, and granola for topping

Instructions:

1. Blend all ingredients in a blender until smooth and creamy. Adjust consistency by adding more milk for thinner or frozen banana for thicker.
2. Taste and adjust sweetness as desired. Honey, maple syrup, or agave nectar are great options.
3. Pour the smoothie mixture into a bowl.
4. Get creative with your green goddess vibes! Arrange fresh apple slices, chopped kale (reserve some for a textural contrast), and granola for a visually appealing and nutrient-packed topping.

Nutritional Information (per serving):

- Calories: 250-300 (depending on ingredients)
- Protein: 5g (with Greek yogurt)
- Carbs: 40g
- Fat: 5g
- Vitamins: A, C, K
- Minerals: Calcium, Iron, Magnesium

Tips & Variations:

- Boost the protein: Add a scoop of protein powder for an extra protein kick.
- Tropical twist: Swap some apple for frozen pineapple or mango for a vibrant flavor fiesta.
- Berry medley: Use a mix of different berries like raspberries or blueberries for a more complex flavor profile.
- Green powerhouse: Add additional leafy greens like spinach or chard for an extra veggie boost.
- Spice it up: Add a pinch of ginger, turmeric, or cinnamon for a warm and flavorful twist.
- Decadent touch: Drizzle with melted dark chocolate or nut butter for a rich and indulgent finish.
- Get creative: Explore different toppings like chia seeds, hemp seeds, shredded coconut, or even edible flowers for added flavor and visual appeal.

Sunny Delight: Mango Peach Smoothie Bowl

Get ready for a taste of summer sunshine with this Sunny Delight: Mango Peach Smoothie Bowl! This vibrant blend of juicy mangoes and sweet peaches creates a flavor explosion that's both refreshing and satisfying. Packed with vitamins and antioxidants, it's a healthy and delicious option for breakfast, a snack, or even a light dessert.

Ingredients (serves 1):

- 1 cup frozen mango chunks
- 1/2 cup frozen peach slices
- 1/4 cup unsweetened almond milk (or your preferred milk)
- 1/4 cup plain Greek yogurt (optional, for extra protein)
- 1 tablespoon chia seeds (optional, for thickening)
- Fresh mango slices, peach slices, and granola for topping

Instructions:

1. In a blender, combine all ingredients and blend until smooth and creamy. Adjust consistency by adding more milk for thinner or frozen fruit for thicker texture.
2. Taste and adjust sweetness as desired. Honey, maple syrup, or agave nectar are great options.
3. Pour the smoothie mixture into a bowl.
4. Unleash your sunny creativity with the toppings! Arrange fresh mango slices, peach slices, and granola for a delightful combination of taste and texture.

Nutritional Information (per serving):

- Calories: 250-300 (depending on ingredients)
- Protein: 5g (with Greek yogurt)
- Carbs: 40g
- Fat: 5g
- Vitamins: A, C
- Minerals: Potassium, Magnesium

Tips & Variations:

- Boost the protein: Add a scoop of protein powder for an extra protein kick.
- Tropical twist: Swap some mango or peach for frozen pineapple for a vibrant flavor fiesta.
- Berry medley: Add a handful of mixed berries like strawberries or blueberries for a more complex flavor profile.
- Green power: Add a handful of spinach or kale to the blend for a hidden veggie boost.
- Spice it up: Add a pinch of ginger, cardamom, or turmeric for a warm and flavorful twist.
- Decadent touch: Drizzle with melted dark chocolate or nut butter for a rich and indulgent finish.
- Get creative: Explore different toppings like chia seeds, hemp seeds, shredded coconut, or even edible flowers for added flavor and visual appeal.

Choco-Peanut Paradise: A Decadent Smoothie Bowl Dream

Dive into a creamy, dreamy haven of chocolate and peanut butter with this Choco-Peanut Paradise Smoothie Bowl! This irresistible combination of rich cocoa and nutty goodness is a flavor explosion that satisfies your sweet tooth while offering a protein-packed start to your day or a guilt-free afternoon snack.

Ingredients (serves 1):

- ½ frozen banana
- ½ cup frozen strawberries (optional, for sweetness and tartness)
- ¼ cup rolled oats
- ¼ cup unsweetened almond milk (or your preferred milk)
- 2 tablespoons unsweetened peanut butter
- 1 tablespoon unsweetened cocoa powder
- Pinch of sea salt
- Fresh strawberries, banana slices, chopped peanuts, and dark chocolate shavings for topping (optional)

Instructions:

1. Blend the frozen banana, frozen strawberries (if using), oats, and almond milk in a blender until smooth.
2. Add peanut butter, cocoa powder, and sea salt. Blend again until fully incorporated and creamy.
3. Taste and adjust sweetness or cocoa intensity as desired. You can add more frozen banana, honey, or maple syrup for sweetness, or adjust the cocoa powder for a stronger chocolate flavor.
4. Pour the smoothie mixture into a bowl.

5. Get creative with your toppings! Arrange fresh strawberries, banana slices, chopped peanuts, and dark chocolate shavings for a visually appealing and texturally exciting bowl.

Nutritional Information (approximate per serving):

- Calories: 350-450 (depending on ingredients)
- Protein: 20g (with added protein powder)
- Carbs: 40g
- Fat: 20g

Tips & Variations:

- Boost the protein: Add a scoop of protein powder for an extra protein kick.
- Go green: Blend in a handful of spinach or kale for a hidden veggie boost.
- Fruity twist: Swap some strawberries for other fruits like blueberries, mango, or pineapple for a different flavor combination.
- Spice it up: Add a pinch of cinnamon, cayenne pepper, or ginger for a unique twist.
- Decadent drizzle: Drizzle with melted dark chocolate, tahini, or even a touch of balsamic glaze for a richer flavor profile.
- Get creative: Explore different toppings like chia seeds, hemp seeds, granola, or even edible flowers for added flavor and visual appeal.

Berrylicious & Creamy: Berry Avocado Smoothie Bowl

This Berrylicious & Creamy: Berry Avocado Smoothie Bowl offers a vibrant and delicious way to fuel your day with healthy fats, vitamins, and antioxidants. The creamy avocado base perfectly complements the tartness of berries, creating a flavor combination that's both refreshing and satisfying.

Ingredients (serves 1):

- 1/2 frozen banana
- 1/2 cup mixed frozen berries (your choice)
- 1/4 ripe avocado, peeled and pitted
- 1/4 cup unsweetened almond milk (or your preferred milk)
- 1/4 cup plain Greek yogurt (optional, for extra protein)
- 1 tablespoon chia seeds (optional, for thickening)
- Fresh berries, granola, and shredded coconut for topping

Instructions:

1. Blend the frozen banana, berries, avocado, and almond milk in a blender until smooth and creamy. Adjust the consistency by adding more milk for thinner or frozen banana for thicker texture.
2. Taste and adjust sweetness as desired. Honey, maple syrup, or agave nectar are great options.
3. Pour the smoothie mixture into a bowl.
4. Get creative with your berrylicious presentation! Arrange fresh berries, granola, and shredded coconut for a delightful explosion of color and texture.

Nutritional Information (per serving):

- Calories: 300-350 (depending on ingredients)
- Protein: 5g (with Greek yogurt)
- Carbs: 40g, Fat: 15g, Vitamins: A, C, E
- Minerals: Potassium, Magnesium

Tips & Variations:

- Boost the protein: Add a scoop of protein powder for an extra protein kick.
- Tropical twist: Swap some berries for frozen pineapple or mango for a vibrant flavor fiesta.
- Green power: Add a handful of spinach or kale to the blend for a hidden veggie boost.
- Spice it up: Add a pinch of ginger, cardamom, or turmeric for a warm and flavorful twist.
- Decadent touch: Drizzle with melted dark chocolate or nut butter for a rich and indulgent finish.
- Get creative: Explore different toppings like chia seeds, hemp seeds, sliced nuts, or even edible flowers for added flavor and visual appeal.
- Chocolate Berry Bliss: Add a tablespoon of unsweetened cocoa powder to the blend for a chocolatey twist. Top with dark chocolate shavings and cacao nibs for added richness.
- Minty Berry Refresh: Blend in a few fresh mint leaves for a refreshing and invigorating flavor. Top with fresh mint sprigs and sliced cucumber for a cool and vibrant experience.
- Creamy Berry Dream: Use full-fat coconut milk for a richer and creamier base. Top with dollops of whipped cream and fresh berries for a decadent treat.

Tropical Escape: Coconut Almond Smoothie Bowl

Immerse yourself in island vibes with this Tropical Escape: Coconut Almond Smoothie Bowl! This creamy blend of coconut and almonds creates a taste of paradise in every spoonful, packed with healthy fats, protein, and vitamins. Perfect for breakfast, a post-workout treat, or a refreshing snack, this smoothie bowl is an invitation to relax and enjoy the moment.

Ingredients (serves 1):

- 1/2 cup unsweetened shredded coconut
- 1/4 cup unsweetened almond milk
- 1/4 cup water
- 1/2 frozen banana
- 1 tablespoon almond butter
- 1/2 teaspoon ground cinnamon (optional)
- Fresh pineapple slices, sliced almonds, and shredded coconut for topping

Instructions:

1. In a blender, combine half of the shredded coconut, almond milk, water, frozen banana, and almond butter. Blend until smooth and creamy.
2. Add the remaining shredded coconut and cinnamon (if using) and blend again until just incorporated.
3. Taste and adjust sweetness or consistency as desired. You can add more frozen banana, honey, or maple syrup for sweetness, or adjust the liquid for a thinner or thicker texture.
4. Pour the smoothie mixture into a bowl.
5. Get ready to embark on your tropical escape! Decorate your bowl with fresh pineapple slices, sliced almonds,

and the remaining shredded coconut for a visually appealing and texturally exciting experience.

Nutritional Information (approximate per serving):

- Calories: 300-350 (depending on ingredients)
- Protein: 10g, Carbs: 30g, Fat: 20g

Tips & Variations:

- Boost the protein: Add a scoop of protein powder for an extra protein kick.
- Berry twist: Swap some pineapple for frozen berries like strawberries or mango for a different flavor combination.
- Green power: Add a handful of spinach or kale to the blend for a hidden veggie boost.
- Spice it up: Add a pinch of ginger, turmeric, or cardamom for a warm and flavorful twist.
- Decadent touch: Drizzle with melted dark chocolate, tahini, or even a touch of balsamic glaze for a richer flavor profile.
- Get creative: Explore different toppings like chia seeds, hemp seeds, granola, or even edible flowers for added flavor and visual appeal.
- Mango Tango: Substitute some pineapple for frozen mango chunks for a vibrant and tropical flavor explosion.
- Chocolate Dream: Add a tablespoon of unsweetened cocoa powder to the blend for a decadent chocolatey twist. Top with dark chocolate shavings and cacao nibs for added richness.
- Creamy Dream: Use full-fat coconut milk instead of water for a thicker and creamier base. Top with dollops of whipped cream and toasted coconut flakes for a luxurious treat.

Zen Oasis: Green Tea & Ginger Smoothie Bowl

Embrace a moment of tranquility with this Zen Oasis: Green Tea & Ginger Smoothie Bowl! This vibrant blend of matcha green tea and fresh ginger creates a refreshingly flavorful and antioxidant-rich experience, perfect for starting your day with a mindful boost or enjoying a light and healthy snack.

Ingredients (serves 1):

- 1/2 cup unsweetened almond milk (or your preferred milk)
- 1/4 cup plain Greek yogurt (optional, for extra protein)
- 1/4 cup spinach or kale
- 1/2 frozen banana
- 1 tablespoon matcha green tea powder
- 1/2 teaspoon grated fresh ginger
- 1/4 cup water (optional, for adjusting consistency)
- Fresh berries, granola, and sliced almonds for topping

Instructions:

- Blend the almond milk, Greek yogurt (if using), spinach or kale, banana, matcha powder, and ginger in a blender until smooth and creamy.
- Adjust the consistency by adding more water if desired.
- Taste and adjust sweetness as desired. Honey, maple syrup, or agave nectar are great options.
- Pour the smoothie mixture into a bowl.
- Find your zen moment with the toppings! Arrange fresh berries, granola, and sliced almonds for a visually appealing and texturally delightful presentation.

Nutritional Information (per serving):

- Calories: 250-300 (depending on ingredients)
- Protein: 5g (with Greek yogurt)
- Carbs: 30g, Fat: 5g, Vitamins: A, C, K
- Minerals: Calcium, Iron, Magnesium

Tips & Variations:

- Boost the protein: Add a scoop of protein powder for an extra protein kick.
- Fruity twist: Swap some berries for other fruits like mango, pineapple, or kiwi for a different flavor combination.
- Tropical touch: Add a few pieces of frozen pineapple or mango for a taste of the tropics.
- Spice it up: Add a pinch of cayenne pepper or turmeric for a warm and invigorating kick.
- Decadent drizzle: Drizzle with tahini, melted dark chocolate, or a touch of honey for a richer flavor profile.
- Get creative: Explore different toppings like chia seeds, hemp seeds, coconut flakes, or even edible flowers for added flavor and visual appeal.
- Mint Mojito Twist: Blend in a few fresh mint leaves for a refreshing and invigorating flavor. Top with fresh mint sprigs and lime wedges for a complete mojito experience.
- Matcha Latte Bowl: For a thicker and creamier bowl, use less water and top with dollops of whipped cream and a sprinkle of matcha powder for a latte-inspired treat.
- Berry Powerhouse: Add a handful of mixed berries to the blend for a hidden boost of antioxidants and a vibrant color.

Tart & Tangy Delight: Blackberry Lemon Smoothie Bowl

Get ready for a vibrant explosion of flavor with this Tart & Tangy Delight: Blackberry Lemon Smoothie Bowl! This refreshing blend of sweet blackberries and zesty lemon creates a taste bud dance in every spoonful, packed with vitamins and antioxidants. Perfect for breakfast, a post-workout treat, or a light snack, this smoothie bowl is a celebration of sunshine and citrusy goodness.

Ingredients (serves 1):

- 1 cup frozen blackberries
- 1/2 frozen banana
- 1/4 cup unsweetened almond milk (or your preferred milk)
- 1/4 cup plain Greek yogurt (optional, for extra protein)
- 1 tablespoon freshly squeezed lemon juice
- 1/2 teaspoon honey or maple syrup (optional, for added sweetness)
- Fresh blackberries, lemon slices, and granola for topping

Instructions:

1. In a blender, combine the frozen blackberries, banana, almond milk, Greek yogurt (if using), lemon juice, and honey (if using).
2. Blend until smooth and creamy, adjusting the consistency by adding more milk for thinner or frozen banana for thicker texture.
3. Taste and adjust sweetness or tartness as desired. You can add more honey or maple syrup for sweetness, or adjust the lemon juice for a stronger tart flavor.

4. Pour the smoothie mixture into a bowl.
5. Unleash your tart and tangy creativity! Arrange fresh blackberries, lemon slices, and granola for a visually appealing and texturally exciting experience.

Nutritional Information (approximate per serving):

- Calories: 250-300 (depending on ingredients)
- Protein: 5g (with Greek yogurt)
- Carbs: 40g
- Fat: 5g
- Vitamins: C, K
- Minerals: Potassium, Manganese

Tips & Variations:

- Boost the protein: Add a scoop of protein powder for an extra protein kick.
- Berry medley: Swap some blackberries for other berries like raspberries, blueberries, or strawberries for a more complex flavor profile.
- Tropical twist: Add a few pieces of frozen pineapple or mango for a taste of the tropics.
- Green power: Add a handful of spinach or kale to the blend for a hidden veggie boost.
- Spice it up: Add a pinch of ginger, turmeric, or cinnamon for a warm and flavorful twist.
- Decadent drizzle: Drizzle with tahini, melted dark chocolate, or a touch of honey for a richer flavor profile.
- Get creative: Explore different toppings like chia seeds, hemp seeds, coconut flakes, or even edible flowers for added flavor and visual appeal.

- Creamy Dream: Use full-fat coconut milk instead of almond milk for a thicker and creamier base. Top with dollops of whipped cream and toasted coconut flakes for a luxurious treat.
- Lemon Zest Surprise: Add a teaspoon of lemon zest along with the lemon juice for an extra burst of citrusy flavor.
- Chia Pudding Base: For a more protein-packed and fiber-rich option, prepare a chia pudding base the night before using almond milk, chia seeds, and a touch of honey. Layer the smoothie mixture on top for a delicious and textured bowl.

Ice Cream Sandwiches

Chocolate Chip Cookie Ice Cream Sandwiches:

A Childhood Dream Come True

Remember the pure joy of biting into a homemade chocolate chip cookie ice cream sandwich? That perfect combination of warm, soft cookies and creamy, cold ice cream is a timeless treat that brings back happy memories for many. Now you can recreate that magic in your own kitchen with this easy and delicious recipe!

Ingredients:

For the Cookies (makes about 12-14 cookies):

- 1 cup (2 sticks) unsalted butter, softened
- 1 cup granulated sugar
- 1 cup packed light brown sugar
- 2 large eggs
- 2 teaspoons pure vanilla extract
- 2 ¾ cups all-purpose flour
- 1 teaspoon baking soda
- 1 teaspoon salt
- 1 ½ cups semisweet chocolate chips

For the Ice Cream:

- Your favorite store-bought or homemade ice cream (we recommend vanilla, chocolate chip cookie dough, or mint chocolate chip!)

Instructions:

1. **Make the Cookies**: Preheat oven to 375°F (190°C). Line baking sheets with parchment paper.
2. In a large bowl, cream together softened butter and sugars until light and fluffy. Beat in eggs one at a time, then stir in vanilla extract.
3. In a separate bowl, whisk together flour, baking soda, and salt. Gradually add dry ingredients to wet ingredients, mixing until just combined. Fold in chocolate chips.
4. Drop rounded tablespoons of dough onto prepared baking sheets, leaving space between each cookie. Bake for 10-12 minutes, or until the edges are golden brown. Let cookies cool completely on wire racks.
5. Assemble the Sandwiches: Once cookies are cool, select two cookies of similar size. Place a generous scoop of ice cream between the two cookies, gently pressing them together to form a sandwich. Repeat with remaining cookies and ice cream.
6. Optional: Wrap each sandwich individually in parchment paper or plastic wrap for easy storage and freezing.

Tips and Variations:

- For chewier cookies, bake for a minute or two less. For crispier cookies, bake for an additional minute or two.
- Get creative with your ice cream flavors! Explore options like strawberry, peanut butter, or coffee for a unique twist.
- Sprinkle the ice cream with chopped nuts, sprinkles, or mini chocolate chips before adding the top cookie for an extra burst of flavor and texture.
- Make it a family activity! Let everyone choose their favorite cookie and ice cream combination to create their own personalized sandwiches.
- For a gourmet touch, drizzle melted chocolate or caramel sauce over the assembled sandwiches before serving.
- If you don't have time to bake cookies, use store-bought ones instead. Just make sure they are the same size and thickness for even ice cream distribution.

Double the Delight: Peanut Butter Cookie Ice Cream Sandwiches

Elevate your childhood classic with the irresistible duo of creamy peanut butter cookies and your favorite ice cream. This recipe takes inspiration from the beloved chocolate chip version, adding a nutty twist for a flavor explosion in every bite.

Ingredients:

For the Cookies (makes about 12-14 cookies):

- 1 cup (2 sticks) unsalted butter, softened
- 1 cup creamy peanut butter
- 1 cup granulated sugar
- 1 cup packed light brown sugar
- 2 large eggs
- 1 teaspoon pure vanilla extract
- 2 ¾ cups all-purpose flour
- 1 teaspoon baking soda
- 1 teaspoon salt

For the Ice Cream:

- Your favorite store-bought or homemade ice cream (chocolate, vanilla, or even strawberry swirl would pair beautifully!)

Instructions:

1. **Make the Cookies:** Preheat oven to 375°F (190°C). Line baking sheets with parchment paper.
2. In a large bowl, cream together softened butter and peanut butter until light and fluffy. Gradually add sugars, beating well after each addition.
3. Beat in eggs one at a time, then stir in vanilla extract.
4. In a separate bowl, whisk together flour, baking soda, and salt. Gradually add dry ingredients to wet ingredients, mixing until just combined.
5. Drop rounded tablespoons of dough onto prepared baking sheets, leaving space between each cookie. Bake for 10-12 minutes, or until the edges are golden brown. Let cookies cool completely on wire racks.
6. Assemble the Sandwiches: Once cookies are cool, select two cookies of similar size. Place a generous scoop of ice cream between the two cookies, gently pressing them together to form a sandwich. Repeat with remaining cookies and ice cream.
7. Optional: Wrap each sandwich individually in parchment paper or plastic wrap for easy storage and freezing.

Tips and Variations:

- For chewier cookies, bake for a minute or two less. For crispier cookies, bake for an additional minute or two.
- Get creative with your ice cream flavors! Explore options like mint chocolate chip, coffee chip, or even a scoop of peanut butter ice cream for a full-on peanut butter dream.

- Drizzle some melted chocolate or caramel sauce over the ice cream before adding the top cookie for an extra layer of decadence.
- Sprinkle the ice cream with chopped peanuts, chocolate chips, or even a pinch of sea salt for added texture and flavor.
- If you don't have time to bake cookies, use store-bought peanut butter cookies instead. Just make sure they are the same size and thickness for even ice cream distribution.
- Make it a family activity! Let everyone choose their favorite ice cream combination to create their own personalized peanut butter cookie ice cream masterpieces.

Chewy & Chunky: Oatmeal Raisin Cookie Ice Cream Sandwiches

Embrace the comforting warmth of oatmeal raisin cookies and the refreshing coolness of your favorite ice cream in this irresistible treat! This recipe combines the classic flavors with the delightful textural contrast of chewy cookies and creamy ice cream, making it a perfect summertime indulgence.

Ingredients:

For the Cookies (makes about 12-14 cookies):

- 1 cup (2 sticks) unsalted butter, softened
- 1 cup packed light brown sugar
- 1 cup granulated sugar
- 2 large eggs
- 2 teaspoons pure vanilla extract
- 1 3/4 cups all-purpose flour
- 1 teaspoon baking soda
- 1/2 teaspoon salt
- 1 1/2 cups rolled oats
- 1 cup raisins

For the Ice Cream:

- Your favorite store-bought or homemade ice cream (vanilla, cinnamon, or even butter pecan would complement the flavors beautifully!)

Instructions:

1. **Make the Cookies**: Preheat oven to 375°F (190°C). Line baking sheets with parchment paper.
2. In a large bowl, cream together softened butter and sugars until light and fluffy. Beat in eggs one at a time, then stir in vanilla extract.
3. In a separate bowl, whisk together flour, baking soda, and salt. Gradually add dry ingredients to wet ingredients, mixing until just combined.
4. Stir in rolled oats and raisins until evenly distributed.
5. Drop rounded tablespoons of dough onto prepared baking sheets, leaving space between each cookie. Bake for 10-12 minutes, or until the edges are golden brown. Let cookies cool completely on wire racks.
6. Assemble the Sandwiches: Once cookies are cool, select two cookies of similar size. Place a generous scoop of ice cream between the two cookies, gently pressing them together to form a sandwich. Repeat with remaining cookies and ice cream.
7. Optional: Wrap each sandwich individually in parchment paper or plastic wrap for easy storage and freezing.

Tips and Variations:

- For chewier cookies, bake for a minute or two less. For crispier cookies, bake for an additional minute or two.
- Get creative with your ice cream flavors! Explore options like coffee, chocolate chip, or even a scoop of cookie dough ice cream for a fun twist.
- Add a sprinkle of cinnamon or nutmeg to the cookie dough for an extra warm and inviting flavor.
- Dip the edges of the cookie in melted chocolate or white chocolate before assembling the sandwiches for an extra decadent touch.
- Toast the rolled oats before adding them to the dough for a deeper flavor and slightly crunchier texture.
- If you don't have raisins, try substituting them with dried cranberries, chopped nuts, or even chocolate chips.
- Make it a family activity! Let everyone choose their preferred ice cream flavor and help assemble their own personalized oatmeal raisin cookie ice cream masterpieces.

Zesty & Refreshing: Lemon Poppy Seed Cookie Ice Cream Sandwiches

Sunshine in a bite! These Lemon Poppy Seed Cookie Ice Cream Sandwiches offer a vibrant and refreshing twist on the classic ice cream sandwich, perfect for brightening up your day. The tangy lemon zest and crunchy poppy seeds in the cookies perfectly complement the creamy sweetness of your chosen ice cream, creating a flavor explosion with every bite.

Ingredients:

- For the Cookies (makes about 12-14 cookies):
- 1 cup (2 sticks) unsalted butter, softened
- 3/4 cup granulated sugar
- 1/2 cup packed light brown sugar
- 1 large egg + 1 egg yolk
- 1 tablespoon lemon zest
- 1 teaspoon pure vanilla extract
- 2 1/4 cups all-purpose flour
- 1/2 teaspoon baking soda
- 1/4 teaspoon salt
- 2 tablespoons poppy seeds

For the Ice Cream:

- Your favorite store-bought or homemade ice cream (lemon, raspberry, or even strawberry would pair beautifully!)

Instructions:

1. Make the Cookies: Preheat oven to 375°F (190°C). Line baking sheets with parchment paper.
2. In a large bowl, cream together softened butter and sugars until light and fluffy. Beat in egg and egg yolk, then stir in lemon zest and vanilla extract.
3. In a separate bowl, whisk together flour, baking soda, and salt. Gradually add dry ingredients to wet ingredients, mixing until just combined. Fold in poppy seeds.
4. Drop rounded tablespoons of dough onto prepared baking sheets, leaving space between each cookie. Bake for 10-12 minutes, or until the edges are golden brown. Let cookies cool completely on wire racks.
5. Assemble the Sandwiches: Once cookies are cool, select two cookies of similar size. Place a generous scoop of ice cream between the two cookies, gently pressing them together to form a sandwich. Repeat with remaining cookies and ice cream.
6. Optional: Wrap each sandwich individually in parchment paper or plastic wrap for easy storage and freezing.

Tips and Variations:

- For chewier cookies, bake for a minute or two less. For crispier cookies, bake for an additional minute or two.
- Get creative with your ice cream flavors! Explore options like blueberry, peach, or even a scoop of lemon sorbet for a truly citrusy experience.
- Drizzle the assembled sandwiches with melted white chocolate or a simple lemon glaze for an extra touch of sweetness and elegance.

- Dip the edges of the cookies in crushed pistachios or chopped candied lemon peel before assembling for a fun textural and visual contrast.
- For a richer flavor, substitute half of the all-purpose flour with almond flour.
- Make it a family activity! Let everyone choose their preferred ice cream flavor and help decorate their own lemon poppy seed cookie ice cream masterpieces with sprinkles, edible flowers, or even a dusting of powdered sugar.

Decadent Dreams: Dark Chocolate Brownie Ice Cream Sandwiches

Indulge in pure chocolate bliss with these Dark Chocolate Brownie Ice Cream Sandwiches! Rich, fudgy brownies meet creamy ice cream for a symphony of textures and flavors that will satisfy even the most intense chocolate cravings. This recipe is an ode to chocolate lovers, offering a homemade touch for an unforgettable treat.

Ingredients:

For the Brownies (makes about 9-12 squares):

- 1 cup (2 sticks) unsalted butter, softened
- 1 cup granulated sugar
- 1 cup packed light brown sugar
- 3 large eggs
- 1 teaspoon pure vanilla extract
- 1 cup unsweetened cocoa powder
- 1 teaspoon baking powder
- 1/2 teaspoon salt
- 1 cup all-purpose flour

For the Ice Cream:

- Your favorite store-bought or homemade ice cream (vanilla, chocolate chip cookie dough, or even mint chocolate chip would be phenomenal!)

Instructions:

1. Make the Brownies: Preheat the oven to 350°F (175°C). Line an 8x8 inch baking pan with parchment paper.
2. In a large bowl, cream together softened butter and sugars until light and fluffy. Beat in eggs one at a time, then stir in vanilla extract.
3. In a separate bowl, whisk together cocoa powder, baking powder, and salt. Gradually add dry ingredients to wet ingredients, mixing until just combined. Stir in flour until fully incorporated.
4. Pour batter into the prepared baking pan and spread evenly. Bake for 25-30 minutes, or until a toothpick inserted into the center comes out with moist crumbs (not completely dry). Let brownies cool completely in the pan on a wire rack.
5. Assemble the Sandwiches: Once brownies are cool, cut them into squares of equal size. Place a generous scoop of ice cream on one brownie square. Top with another brownie square, gently pressing down to form a sandwich. Repeat with remaining brownies and ice cream.
6. Optional: Wrap each sandwich individually in parchment paper or plastic wrap for easy storage and freezing. You can also drizzle them with melted dark chocolate or caramel sauce for an extra decadent touch.

Tips and Variations:

- For fudgier brownies, bake for a minute or two less. For cakier brownies, bake for an additional minute or two.
- Get creative with your ice cream flavors! Explore options like coffee, strawberry, or even a scoop of peanut butter ice cream for a delightful flavor combination.
- Sprinkle the ice cream with chopped nuts, chocolate chips, or sea salt before adding the top brownie for an extra burst of flavor and texture.
- Instead of square brownies, use heart-shaped cookie cutters to create adorable and festive sandwiches for Valentine's Day or other special occasions.
- Make it a family activity! Let everyone choose their preferred ice cream flavor and help assemble their own personalized dark chocolate brownie ice cream masterpieces.

Classic & Refreshing: Vanilla Wafer Ice Cream Sandwiches

These Vanilla Wafer Ice Cream Sandwiches offer a nostalgic and simple treat, perfect for satisfying sweet cravings with minimal fuss. The crisp, delicate vanilla wafers perfectly complement the creamy ice cream, creating a refreshing and delightful bite in every sandwich.

Ingredients:

- 1 box Vanilla Wafers (approximately 24-30 wafers)
- 1 container (1 pint) of your favorite ice cream (vanilla, chocolate, strawberry, or any flavor you love!)
- Optional: Toppings such as sprinkles, chocolate sauce, chopped nuts, or whipped cream

Instructions:

1. Gather your ingredients: Ensure your ice cream is softened slightly for easier scooping. If it's frozen solid, let it sit at room temperature for about 10-15 minutes.
2. Prepare your workspace: Have a flat surface ready for assembling the sandwiches and a plate or tray lined with parchment paper for storing them if desired.
3. Assemble the sandwiches: Choose two vanilla wafers of similar size. Place a generous scoop of ice cream between the wafers, gently pressing them together to form a sandwich. Repeat with remaining wafers and ice cream.
4. Get creative (optional): If desired, drizzle with melted chocolate sauce, caramel sauce, or top with sprinkles, chopped nuts, or whipped cream for an extra layer of flavor and fun.

5. Enjoy immediately: Serve the sandwiches right away for the perfect balance of crisp wafers and creamy ice cream.

Tips & Variations:

- For a thicker ice cream layer, use larger scoops or cookies.
- Freeze the assembled sandwiches for 30 minutes before serving for an extra firm and refreshing treat.
- Get creative with wafer flavors! Explore options like chocolate, strawberry, or even mint flavored wafers for a different taste experience.
- Make it a sundae bar! Set up a variety of toppings and let everyone create their own personalized vanilla wafer ice cream sundae masterpiece.
- For a healthier twist, use whole wheat or gluten-free vanilla wafers.
- Make it a family activity! Gather your loved ones and have fun assembling these classic ice cream sandwiches together.

Sweet, Summery Bliss: Strawberry Shortcake Ice Cream Sandwiches

Embrace the taste of summer with these delightful Strawberry Shortcake Ice Cream Sandwiches! This recipe combines the fresh sweetness of strawberries, airy biscuits, and creamy ice cream, creating a delightful treat that's perfect for picnics, parties, or simply enjoying a sunny afternoon.

Ingredients:

For the Biscuits (makes about 8 servings):

- 1 1/2 cups all-purpose flour
- 2 tablespoons granulated sugar
- 2 teaspoons baking powder
- 1/2 teaspoon salt
- 1/4 cup cold unsalted butter, cubed
- 1/2 cup cold milk (buttermilk for extra tang)

For the Strawberries:

- 2 cups fresh strawberries, sliced
- 1/4 cup granulated sugar (optional, adjust to taste)

For the Ice Cream:

- 1 pint your favorite ice cream (vanilla, strawberry, or even lemon would complement the flavors beautifully!)

Instructions:

Make the Biscuits:

1. Preheat oven to 425°F (220°C). Line a baking sheet with parchment paper.
2. In a large bowl, whisk together flour, sugar, baking powder, and salt. Using a pastry cutter or your fingers, cut in the cold butter until the mixture resembles coarse crumbs.
3. Stir in milk just until a dough forms. Avoid overmixing.
4. Gently pat the dough into a 1-inch thick circle on a lightly floured surface.
5. Cut out biscuits using a 2-inch round cutter or a drinking glass.
6. Place biscuits on the prepared baking sheet, leaving space between them. Bake for 10-12 minutes, or until golden brown and cooked through. Let cool completely on a wire rack.

Prepare the Strawberries:

*   Slice the strawberries and toss them with sugar, if desired. Let them sit for a few minutes to release their juices.

Assemble the Sandwiches:

*   Once the biscuits are cool, split them in half horizontally.
*   Place a generous scoop of ice cream on the bottom half of a biscuit.
*   Top with a layer of sliced strawberries.
*   Place the top half of the biscuit on top, gently pressing down to form a sandwich.
*   Repeat with remaining biscuits, ice cream, and strawberries.

Serve & Enjoy:

- Serve the sandwiches immediately for a perfect balance of warm biscuits, cold ice cream, and juicy strawberries.
- If desired, drizzle with melted chocolate sauce, caramel sauce, or a simple strawberry glaze for an extra touch of sweetness.

Tips & Variations:

- For softer biscuits, brush them with melted butter before baking.
- Get creative with your ice cream flavors! Explore options like chocolate chip cookie dough, mint chocolate chip, or even a scoop of strawberry sorbet for a lighter option.
- Add a dollop of whipped cream or mascarpone cheese on top of the ice cream for extra richness.
- For a fun twist, use mini biscuits and create bite-sized ice cream sandwiches.
- Make it a family activity! Let everyone assemble their own personalized strawberry shortcake ice cream masterpieces with their favorite toppings.

Golden & Gooey: Chocolate Chunk Blondie Ice Cream Sandwiches

Get ready to dive into pure indulgence with these Chocolate Chunk Blondie Ice Cream Sandwiches! Rich, chewy blondies studded with melty chocolate chunks meet creamy ice cream, creating a flavor and texture explosion in every bite. This recipe offers a delicious twist on the classic ice cream sandwich, perfect for satisfying your sweet tooth with a homemade touch.

Ingredients:

For the Blondies (makes about 9-12 squares):

- 1 cup (2 sticks) unsalted butter, softened
- 3/4 cup packed light brown sugar
- 1/2 cup granulated sugar
- 2 large eggs
- 1 teaspoon pure vanilla extract
- 1 cup all-purpose flour
- 1/2 teaspoon baking powder
- 1/4 teaspoon salt
- 1 cup semisweet chocolate chips

For the Ice Cream:

- Your favorite store-bought or homemade ice cream (chocolate chip cookie dough, vanilla bean, or even peanut butter would be amazing!)

Instructions:

1. **Make the Blondies**: Preheat oven to 350°F (175°C). Line an 8x8 inch baking pan with parchment paper.
2. In a large bowl, cream together softened butter and sugars until light and fluffy. Beat in eggs one at a time, then stir in vanilla extract.
3. In a separate bowl, whisk together flour, baking powder, and salt. Gradually add dry ingredients to wet ingredients, mixing until just combined. Fold in chocolate chips.
4. Pour batter into the prepared baking pan and spread evenly. Bake for 20-25 minutes, or until the edges are golden brown and a toothpick inserted in the center comes out with moist crumbs. Let blondies cool completely in the pan on a wire rack.
5. Assemble the Sandwiches: Once blondies are cool, cut them into squares of equal size. Place a generous scoop of ice cream on one blondie square. Top with another blondie square, gently pressing down to form a sandwich. Repeat with remaining blondies and ice cream.
6. Optional: Wrap each sandwich individually in parchment paper or plastic wrap for easy storage and freezing. You can also drizzle them with melted chocolate or caramel sauce for an extra decadent touch.

Tips & Variations:

- For chewier blondies, bake for a minute or two less. For cakier blondies, bake for an additional minute or two.
- Get creative with your ice cream flavors! Explore options like mint chocolate chip, cookies and cream, or even a scoop of chocolate-covered cherry ice cream for a fun surprise.
- Sprinkle the ice cream with chopped nuts, sea salt, or even a drizzle of melted peanut butter before adding the top blondie for an extra burst of flavor and texture.
- Instead of square blondies, use heart-shaped cookie cutters to create adorable and festive sandwiches for Valentine's Day or other special occasions.
- Make it a family activity! Let everyone choose their preferred ice cream flavor and help assemble their own personalized chocolate chunk blondie ice cream masterpieces.

Pumpkin Spice Cookie Ice Cream Sandwiches

Ingredients:

For the Pumpkin Spice Cookies (makes about 12-14 cookies):
- 1 cup (2 sticks) unsalted butter, softened
- 1 cup granulated sugar
- 1 cup packed light brown sugar
- 2 large eggs
- 1 teaspoon pure vanilla extract
- 2 ¾ cups all-purpose flour
- 1 teaspoon baking soda
- 1 teaspoon salt
- 1 ½ teaspoons pumpkin pie spice
- ½ teaspoon ground cinnamon
- ½ teaspoon ground ginger
- ¼ teaspoon ground nutmeg
- ½ cup semisweet chocolate chips

For the Ice Cream:

- Your favorite store-bought or homemade pumpkin spice ice cream (or any flavor you like!)

Instructions:

1. **Make the Cookies**: Preheat oven to 375°F (190°C). Line baking sheets with parchment paper.
2. In a large bowl, cream together softened butter and sugars until light and fluffy. Beat in eggs one at a time, then stir in vanilla extract.
3. In a separate bowl, whisk together flour, baking soda, salt, pumpkin pie spice, cinnamon, ginger, and nutmeg. Gradually add dry ingredients to wet ingredients, mixing until just combined. Fold in chocolate chips.

4. Drop rounded tablespoons of dough onto prepared baking sheets, leaving space between each cookie. Bake for 10-12 minutes, or until the edges are golden brown. Let cookies cool completely on wire racks.

5. Assemble the Sandwiches: Once cookies are cool, select two cookies of similar size. Place a generous scoop of ice cream between the two cookies, gently pressing them together to form a sandwich. Repeat with remaining cookies and ice cream.

6. Optional: Wrap each sandwich individually in parchment paper or plastic wrap for easy storage and freezing.

Tips and Variations:

- For chewier cookies, bake for a minute or two less. For crispier cookies, bake for an additional minute or two.
- Get creative with your ice cream flavors! Explore options like vanilla, chocolate chip cookie dough, or even a scoop of maple walnut ice cream for a comforting fall flavor.
- Spice up the cookies! Add a pinch of cayenne pepper to the dough for a subtle kick.
- Drizzle the assembled sandwiches with melted chocolate or caramel sauce for an extra decadent touch.
- Sprinkle the ice cream with chopped nuts, pumpkin seeds, or a sprinkle of cinnamon sugar before adding the top cookie for an extra layer of flavor and texture.
- Use store-bought pumpkin spice cookie dough to save time.
- Make it a family activity! Let everyone choose their favorite ice cream flavor and help assemble their own personalized pumpkin spice cookie ice cream masterpieces.

Red Velvet Cake Ice Cream Sandwiches: A Decadent Treat with Nutrition Insights

These delightful Red Velvet Cake Ice Cream Sandwiches are the perfect indulgence for any chocolate lover. Rich, moist red velvet cake pairs beautifully with creamy ice cream, creating a taste and texture explosion in every bite. While it's a treat to be enjoyed occasionally, let's dive into the recipe and explore its nutritional value.

Ingredients:

For the Red Velvet Cake (makes about 9-12 squares):
- 1 1/2 cups all-purpose flour
- 1 tablespoon unsweetened cocoa powder
- 1 teaspoon baking soda
- 1/2 teaspoon salt
- 1 cup (2 sticks) unsalted butter, softened
- 1 1/2 cups granulated sugar
- 2 large eggs
- 1 teaspoon pure vanilla extract
- 1 teaspoon red food coloring
- 1 cup buttermilk

For the Ice Cream:

- 1 quart your favorite ice cream (vanilla, chocolate chip, or even strawberry would complement the flavors beautifully!)

Instructions:

1. **Make the Red Velvet Cake**: Preheat the oven to 350°F (175°C). Line an 8x8 inch baking pan with parchment paper.
2. In a medium bowl, whisk together flour, cocoa powder, baking soda, and salt.
3. In a large bowl, cream together softened butter and sugar until light and fluffy. Beat in eggs one at a time, then stir in vanilla extract and red food coloring.
4. Alternately add the dry ingredients and buttermilk to the wet ingredients, mixing until just combined.
5. Pour batter into the prepared baking pan and spread evenly. Bake for 25-30 minutes, or until a toothpick inserted into the center comes out with moist crumbs. Let the cake cool completely in the pan on a wire rack.
6. Assemble the Sandwiches: Once the cake is cool, cut it into squares of equal size. Place a generous scoop of ice cream on one cake square. Top with another cake square, gently pressing down to form a sandwich. Repeat with remaining cake and ice cream.
7. Optional: Wrap each sandwich individually in parchment paper or plastic wrap for easy storage and freezing.

Nutrition Value:

- Calories: 450-500 (depending on chosen ice cream)
- Fat: 20-25g
- Carbohydrates: 60-70g
- Sugar: 40-50g
- Fiber: 2-3g
- Protein: 5-10g

Tips and Variations:

- For a healthier cake option, use reduced-fat ingredients and substitute half of the all-purpose flour with whole wheat flour.
- Get creative with your ice cream flavors! Explore options like mint chocolate chip, coffee chip, or even a scoop of cheesecake ice cream for a delightful twist.
- Make it a family activity! Let everyone choose their favorite ice cream flavor and help assemble their own personalized red velvet cake ice cream masterpieces.

Chapter 5:

Sweet Endings & Beyond

We'll explore how to elevate your frozen treats from simple snacks to Instagram-worthy creations. We'll provide creative topping ideas and plating suggestions to make your frozen treats the highlight of any meal or dessert table.

Presentation Perfection

The key to an Instagram-worthy frozen treat is all in the presentation. By using unique and colorful garnishes, fun and creative serving dishes, and eye-catching plating techniques, you can turn your frozen treats into a visual masterpiece. Here are some ideas to help you achieve presentation perfection:

Creative Topping Ideas

- Sprinkle fresh herbs like mint, basil, or lavender over your frozen treats for a pop of color and a refreshing flavor.
- Add a drizzle of caramel, chocolate sauce, or fruit coulis to add a touch of sweetness and a decorative touch.
- Top your frozen treats with edible flowers like lavender, pansies, or violets for a pop of color and an elegant finish.
- Sprinkle chopped nuts like almonds, pistachios, or walnuts over your frozen treats for a crunchy texture and a nutty flavor.
- Add a sprinkle of edible glitter or shimmer powder for a festive and sparkly finish.

Fun and Creative Serving Dishes

1. Serve your frozen treats in fun and colorful dishes like Mason jars, mugs, or small bowls.
2. Use unique serving dishes like waffle cones, coconut bowls, or hollowed-out fruit like pineapple or watermelon.
3. Serve your frozen treats in clear glasses or glasses with decorative stems to showcase their beauty.
4. Use cute and colorful serving dishes like ice cream cones, popsicle molds, or small jars to create individual servings.
5. Eye-Catching Plating Techniques
6. Create a decorative swirl of your frozen treat on the plate using a spoon or spatula.
7. Serve your frozen treats in a tower, stacking different flavors and textures on top of each other for a visually appealing presentation.
8. Use a variety of colors and textures in your frozen treats, like chocolate and vanilla, or fruit and nuts, to create a beautiful contrast on the plate.
9. Garnish your frozen treats with fresh fruit, whipped cream, or sprinkles to add a pop of color and a sweet finish.

By using creative topping ideas, fun and creative serving dishes, and eye-catching plating techniques, you can turn your frozen treats into a masterpiece that is as beautiful to look at as it is delicious to eat.

Sweet Inspiration

While frozen treats are a delightful indulgence, they can also be incorporated into a healthy and balanced lifestyle. Here are some tips for incorporating your homemade frozen treats into meal plans and maintaining a healthy lifestyle:

Planning Ahead

One way to ensure that your frozen treats fit into your meal plan is to plan ahead. Think about what other meals and snacks you'll be having throughout the day and consider how your frozen treat will fit into your overall calorie and nutrient needs. If you're planning on having a heavier meal, you might want to opt for a lighter frozen treat, like a sorbet or a fruit-based yogurt bowl. If you've had a lighter day overall, you might choose to indulge in a richer frozen treat like a chocolate ice cream or a cookie sandwich.

Portion Control

Another way to incorporate frozen treats into a healthy lifestyle is to practice portion control. Instead of eating an entire pint of ice cream in one sitting, try portioning out your frozen treats into individual servings and freezing them for later. This way, you can enjoy a frozen treat as a sweet and satisfying snack without overindulging.

Mindful Indulgence

Remember that indulging in a frozen treat from time to time can be part of a balanced and healthy lifestyle. By making your own frozen treats using the Ninja Creami Deluxe, you have control over the ingredients, ensuring that you're using high-quality, natural ingredients and avoiding added sugars and preservatives.

Adding Nutrients

To make your frozen treats more nutritious, consider adding nutrient-dense ingredients like nuts, seeds, and fruits. Nuts and seeds are a great source of healthy fats, protein, and fiber, while fruits add natural sweetness and a burst of vitamins and minerals. Adding these ingredients to your frozen treats can help boost their nutritional value and make them more satisfying and filling.

Mindful Eating

Finally, remember to enjoy your frozen treats mindfully. Eating mindfully means paying attention to the taste, texture, and aroma of your frozen treat, savoring each bite, and enjoying the experience of eating it. This can help you feel more satisfied with smaller portions and prevent you from overindulging.

By planning ahead, practicing portion control, adding nutrients, and eating mindfully, you can incorporate your homemade frozen treats into a healthy and balanced lifestyle.

Final Words & Gratitude

Thank you for embarking on this journey with me to explore the world of frozen treats. I hope that this book has inspired you to create your own delicious and healthy frozen treats using the Ninja Creami Deluxe. Remember that the possibilities are endless when it comes to creating frozen treats that are both nutritious and delicious.

I want to express my gratitude to you, the reader, for your curiosity and enthusiasm for making homemade frozen treats. I hope that you will continue to explore and experiment with different ingredients and flavors to create frozen treats that are unique and satisfying.

As you embark on your own journey of frozen delight, remember to have fun and enjoy the process. Don't be afraid to experiment and try new things, and always prioritize using high-quality, natural ingredients.

Happy freezing!
Avery Stoneheart.

Printed in Great Britain
by Amazon

41239317R00096